American Buddha

Stuart Mooney

1st WORLD

PUBLISHING

American Buddha

Stuart Mooney

© Stuart Mooney 2007

Published by 1stWorld Publishing
1100 North 4th St. Fairfield, Iowa 52556
tel: 641-209-5000 • fax: 641-209-3001
web: www.1stworldpublishing.com

First Edition

LCCN: 2007931204
SoftCover ISBN: 978-1-4218-9990-9
HardCover ISBN: 978-1-4218-9991-6
eBook ISBN: 978-1-4218-9992-3

"How do you lead people to something that does not exist, yet is the very goal of existence? How do you lead people to something that language cannot be used to express? How do you lead people to something that is right in front of them, yet is invisible? How do you lead people to something that is worthless, yet worth everything? How do you lead people to something that has no path and no goal? How do you lead people to a place that they can never get to, yet is their only true home? That is the question."

Foreword

To the reader,

I just wanted to thank you in advance for reading my book, *American Buddha*. Through it, I wanted to share my experience with the world. I wanted to share the Divinity that I have been living with the world. I want people to know that it is possible for anyone, anywhere to live in a state of Grace. For its survival, our society has to evolve to the point where the state of Oneness or Unity is a living reality for large numbers of people. I wanted to demystify the experience and to make it palatable for westerners. It is a REAL experience. Awakening is not just something you read about in books. It is a living reality which permeates every breath I take. It is a state of immense freedom yet, at the same time, it is a practical experience. So action is efficient. Fear is gone. There are no boundaries. There is no more gap between subject and object to overcome. Now, subject and object experience each other in greatest ecstasy. The experience is so intensely personal. I now realize that there has only ever been one living being. It is God. It is Oneness. I am Oneness. We are all just that Oneness. How could I ever again harm anyone? They are my body. How could I damage my beautiful earth anymore? Earth is my body. We must move towards this as a species. It is the only solution to our problems. So I will end with an expression of my deep appreciation for your time. If you have any questions, you may contact me through my website at **americanbuddha.net.**

With all Love

Stuart Mooney

Dedication

Helen Lutes was one of those people who just melted into the fabric of American middle-class society. She was a sweet, cookie baking, little old lady from Pasadena. But there was another side to her that few were aware of. Helen Lutes was a fully God-Realized human being. This was the Helen I knew. For more than 20 years, Helen and I engaged in the most extraordinary spiritual relationship. She was my guide. Though I have traveled the world and have interacted with many Yogis, Avatars and other Divine Beings, the truth is that Helen Lutes was the most powerful human being I have ever met. The most fascinating fact is that our entire relationship occurred over the phone. I never actually met Helen. She was a sweet voice, with a touch of a southern drawl, on the other end of the phone line. Helen had the uncanny gift of being able to speak to you on your own level. Whether your level of spiritual development was "kindergarden" or "Ph.D", she was right there with you. Nothing was off limits in our conversations. She once told me that if I could think of the question, no matter what it was, she would answer it. Our conversations ranged from the most subtle analysis of the nature of the Divine, to the utterly mundane. She would be speaking about

Archangels one minute and about how to make a good chicken casserole the next. Helen was always teaching by example. She taught me the value of Practical Divinity. She would never allow me to become a "space cadet". In her last days, Helen asked me to write a book sharing my experiences. "American Buddha" is dedicated to this extraordinary individual.

Shortly before her passing, Helen talked to me one last time. She was very weak and her voice was barely audible. At the end of our conversation, Helen told me that this would be the last time we would ever speak. She then asked me to close my eyes and listen to her voice. She told me that after she stopped speaking, I was to hang up the phone. Then she began to whisper a phrase over and over again. She whispered:

"God and I are One. God and I are One. God and I are One."

Introduction

There are many wonderful books written these days about personal fulfillment. A walk through any bookstore will confirm this. And it is amazes me how many people have found the answer and how many answers there are to the same question. And what is the question? What can I do to end my own suffering? Really, this is the fundamental question of existence. The Buddha recognized this 1500 years ago. The Buddha concluded that life was "Dukka". He concluded that life, in its essence, was suffering. His solution was to identify the cause of suffering. He felt that craving was the cause. The Buddha felt that if he didn't crave for things, then he would not be disappointed and therefore, he would not suffer. Even before the Buddha, the Vedic seers of Ancient India set out to find a solution to suffering and they came up with a number of spiritual technologies to address it. Most of these approaches required withdrawal from life, though, so they were not very useful to society as a whole. Today, thousands of years later, the masses still continue to suffer and we are still searching for a solution to that age old question, "What can I do to end my own suffering"?

American Buddha was written to help shift the reader into

an Awakened Consciousness. American Buddha literally means "Practical Awakening". American Buddha is a state of being, where one is able to enjoy the ancient revelatory consciousness of a Buddha or a Christ, while living comfortably in the modern world. Usually, these two states are considered mutually exclusive. Why? Awakening is the product of an Eastern Mystical culture. Over time, the true knowledge of Awakening has become shrouded in austere rituals and a myriad of complicated techniques. The result is that most, but not all, holy men and women, saints, sadhus, etc., are uncomfortable living in modern society. Now the higher states that they are experiencing are heavenly. They are beyond any earthly pleasures. The problem is that most individuals in these states don't live a "householder" lifestyle. What I mean by this is that they don't have families to raise. They don't have homes with mortgage payments. They don't have 9 to 5 jobs. In fact, they don't participate in the societal drama at all. This is non-productive for our world. We need Awakened farmers, firemen and fry cooks. We need an Awakened society. The purpose of American Buddha is to merge modern material prosperity with Buddhahood. One should not exclude the other.

American Buddha is written in the form of a Divine dialogue between a teacher and his students. There are many aspects of the Awakened experience that are being made available to the reader for the first time in this book. On the deepest level, American Buddha is simply your Soul speaking to itself. The words are just a cover. The words are there just to pacify your mind. It is not the words; rather, it is the state that they will bring you to that is important. These words are a kind of gateway. There is a silence associated with them that is significant. If they are read, just know that you will gain a foothold in the area beyond your mind. You will come to know your Soul intimately. You will come to know your inmost Self. You will taste eternity. You will gradually awaken from a million lifetimes of sleep and you will know your

Divinity. In the end, you will come to live the wisdom of the Saints from time immemorial.

Who Am I

My name is Stuart Mooney and, for more than 35 years, I have taught yogic meditation throughout the world. I have lectured on the subject of "Meditation and the Nature of Higher Consciousness" at more than 100 major Colleges and Universities. Over the years, I have been authorized to teach more than 100 esoteric (privately held) meditation techniques. While I was living in India, an ability to heal and to transmit Shakti spontaneously manifested. This Shakti or Grace was transmitted to thousands at the ancient temples throughout South India. I have been trained to transmit the Oneness Blessing under the guidance of the reknown Avatars, Amma and Bhagwan. I have also been authorized to transmit Knowledge under the authority of the Shankaracharya of South India. I was a lecturer in Psychology at the University of Madras as well as at the Police Training College in Chennai, India. I also saw patients at the Banyan Hospital in Chennai. I have studied, extensively, with the Brahmin Priests of South India and have assisted in the performance of over 700 Vedic Rituals. Those are my credentials. That is what I look like on paper. Now, I want to introduce you to the true me.

In 2004, I underwent a spontaneous shift in consciousness, which has afforded me deep insight into the experiential nature the Awakened Consciousness. I am a pragmatic, rational individual who has undergone a dramatically transformational experience. I am not interested in philosophizing. I am here to express the nature of Divinity. I claim nothing for myself. I do not believe in labels. I am not enlightened, awakened or a guru. I am not in Satori, Nirvana, or Samadhi. I am. I exist.

That's it. That is my only true biography.

Who Are You

It is essential that you understand what is going on. What is happening to you right now is your only reality and you cannot do a single thing to change it. You are not responsible for it and no amount of personal effort can help. There are reasons for this. First, your mind, the one that you identify with, is not your personal mind. Your mind actually exists outside of you. Your mind is just your thoughts. If there are no thoughts, there is no mind. Your thoughts are not yours. They can originate from any possible source. They can come from your genes; your birth or childhood traumas; the weather and/or from the thoughts of any of the 6 billion people alive today. They can even come from those who have long since departed. Your mind is just a pipe. Your mind receives thoughts. So you are not the source of your own thoughts. You are just the experiencer. Your mind has no relationship to "you". Thoughts and the mind are an ancient construct. They will always exist as a part of your experience. No amount of effort can ever eradicate them. Second, your body, the one that you experience through is not yours. The heart beats; the lungs fill; the cells repair themselves; and the baby is created completely independently of your conscious attention. The body acts autonomously. It is not yours.

So if you are not your mind; your thoughts or your body, then, who are you? You might reply that you are the person who is reading this. But if you read this again tomorrow, would the same person be reading it? Do you always have the same point of view? Is there a common thread holding these points of view or these personalities together? The answer is no. The truth is that we are a bunch of individual personalities that rise up and then recede seamlessly into the next one. We have no core personality. Rather, we are many fluid personalities.

If I am not my thoughts, my mind, my body or a fixed personality, who am I? If I am just a bunch of personalities which come and go like the wind, who is left? Who is experiencing? Who is going to have goals and roles? Who is driven to achieve more and more? How can growth be measured without a fixed identity that experiences change?

And who gets Awakened? My thoughts and my mind cannot be Awakened. My body is not me. It cannot participate in my Awakening. My personality is actually made up of many, many fluid personalities which have no common thread. How do I go about Awakening an infinite number of personalities? I can't even Awaken one of them.

The truth is that there is no me. I am just experience. I own nothing and this world is happening without any rhyme or reason. Who gets Awakened? There is no "who", therefore, there is no one to get Awakened. There is no identity to liberate. No human effort can be used to liberate us from what was never there to begin with.

We have all been running frantically after something that does not exist. We are powerless and anything we do from our side is like trying to save ourselves from drowning by grabbing our own shirt and lifting. Only Grace can save us. Something from the other side must lift us out. Without Grace, there is no way to get out of our dream. Grace is light. Grace is not of this world. No set of actions can create Grace because Grace is independent of action. How do we receive Grace then? The following section contains a series of personal stories which will help to reader to open to the nature and power of Divine Grace.

Chapter 1
GRACE

Healing Miracle I

Once I was asked to present a lecture to a group of Psychiatrists at a very prestigious hospital in India. The general topic that I was given was "Mind/Body Medicine". After a couple of hours of speaking, I could see that my audience was looking very bored. Finally, I began to discuss spiritual healing and I asked for a volunteer from the audience. I wanted to show the effects of "spiritual healing" on a trained "neutral" observer. My volunteer was a Social Worker with years of experience. I placed my palms on her head and she immediately jumped. She reported a pleasant tingling sensation radiating throughout her body and the others clapped in approval. The Psychiatrist in Chief, an open minded clinician, expressed great interest and asked me if I would work on a patient of his choosing. After some time, the doors of the auditorium swung open. A tiny lady came into the room escorted by two orderlies. I motioned for her to be seated. I knew that she spoke only Tamil so any communication would be difficult. Through an interpreter, I asked her to close her eyes and cautioned her that I would be placing my palms on her head. I spent perhaps five minutes with her after which she got up and left the room, seeming unaffected. The evening ended and I went back to my room. About nine the next morning, I received a call from the hospital. It was the Psychiatrist In Chief on the line. He told me that the patient that I had worked on the night before was severely Catatonic and had been non verbal for years. He went on to say that she got up on her own for the first time this morning and came to breakfast. He said she was talking up a blue streak and wondered where she had been. Her symptoms had completely disappeared overnight. The Psychiatrists could offer no clinical explanation. They agreed that a miracle had occurred. Even months later, her symptoms remained completely resolved. By the way, the hospital was so excited that they immediately offered me a staff position. They wanted me to heal patients on a regular basis.

This is just one of many, many healing stories. They are all stories of Grace. Because Grace is not logical, sequential, or relegated to formal treatment system, it is not utilized on a regular basis. There is no treatment more effective than Grace because it is Grace, not the specific treatment, which ultimately heals the patient.

Healing Miracle II

When my healing abilities first developed, I was living in an Ashram on the outskirts of the seaport city of Chennai, India. One day, one of the house maids was brought to my room by our cook Amma. The two ladies looked very worried.

Amma pointed to the house maid's neck. On the side of her neck was a golf ball sized lump. I was told, through an interpreter, that it was a cancer and that it was deemed inoperable. I was told she had no husband and three little children. They asked me to heal her. I placed my hand on her neck and kept it there for a few minutes. I remember how hot and pulsating the lump on her neck was. My hand and arm became hot and achy as well. I finished up and I did not see the woman again for about a week. The next time I saw her, she was smiling ear to ear and ran up and pointed to her neck. The lump had been reduced in size. It was perhaps the size of a marble now. Within one month the lump had vanished without leaving even a mark. Over the next year, she invited me to her humble little hut for tea many times. I became close to her children. This event has always served to remind me how deeply Grace can transform lives and that I am so appreciative to have been allowed to participate in such a blessed event.

Healing Miracle III

One day I was seeing clients at my office in Chennai. This lovely old couple walked in. The husband's arm was wrapped carefully around his wife. She seemed very frail and appeared quite sedated. The husband proceeded to relate a story of how his wife had suffered a "nervous breakdown". She had regressed into a psychotic state in which she had not uttered a sound in years. He had to do everything for her. He washed, dressed and fed her. He had come to me because he was under tremendous stress from being the sole caregiver. He wanted me to teach him a deep meditation technique to help him relax. I went ahead and provided him instructions for a mantra meditation technique. I remember that I was repeating the ancient mantra "Wa Si Si Va" out loud and was having the husband repeat it with me. I was about to have him repeat it mentally as a thought when suddenly, the wife started to chant the mantra with us. Her voice was so beautiful. You have no idea how powerful that moment was. The astonished husband looked at her smiling radiant face. He immediately broke into tears. She stood up and performed a puja, (a Hindu ritual of gratitude) with me and they went home in a state of incredible joy. I still can't believe it but it happened. Grace intervened. Grace somehow opened the gates of her brain chemistry and allowed her to connect to her world again.

Healing Miracle IV

When I was living in India, I had a number of internet clients from all over the world. These were people with a lot of pre-existing emotional and spiritual issues. There was one incident in particular I want to share. There was a lady in Toronto. She was a wealthy Chinese professional person who had immigrated to Canada a couple of years before. She had become very depressed and had even mentioned suicide as an alternative. No matter what was suggested, she did not seem to be responding well and I was very concerned. One night, I awoke in a cold sweat. Something told me that I should e-mail this woman immediately. I knew exactly what I wanted to say. I e-mailed the following: "Don't do it! God does not want you to do it!" Then I pushed the send button and went back to sleep. I did not hear from her for a day or two. This is how she finally responded. She told me that she had decided to kill herself and she was on her way to the kitchen to get a knife and slit her wrists. As she walked by her computer the little "You've got mail" sound went off and she reluctantly decided to open the mail. Of course, it was my e-mail telling her not to do it. She was so stunned by the timing of the event that she was certain that it was sent directly from God. The experience transformed her and she went on to marry and to have a very successful business career. This is just another example of how Grace carries the power to change a destiny in an instant.

Miracle Manifestation I

Many times people would come to see me with very specific requests. They needed something right away. Here is an example. One day, a couple visited me at my office in Chennai. It seems that they were both school teachers who had been offered teaching positions in Atlanta, Georgia in the U. S. Unfortunately, this was post 9/11 and it was very difficult for Indian nationals to obtain the proper visas to travel to the U.S. This poor couple had been waiting for more than a year. They had given up their lucrative teaching jobs in Chennai and sold their house assuming that they would be leaving shortly. When I saw them, they were desperate and almost out of money. They asked me for a technique to help them manifest their desire to go to the U. S. I had them sit and close their eyes. Then I asked them put attention at the third eye (between the eyebrows). I asked them to picture a bright light there. Then I asked them each to imagine going to their mailbox where they lived and opening a letter. The letter contained their new travel visas. I had them place this image in their third eye and fill the image with a bright white light. This was at 11 o'clock in the morning. That evening, I was giving a lecture when my interpreter pulled me aside. He told me that the couple had just called. He said that they had come home and checked their mailbox only to find the letter with their travel visas just as they had pictured in my office. The question is, did the visas create the need for the mental image in my office or did the mental image in my office create the visas? The answer is that Grace created a synchronicity. Who cares whether the chicken or the egg came first.

Miracle Manifestation II

One half hour after the couple from the Miracle Manifestation I story left my office, a second couple came to see me. They had another sad story. They too were desperate. It seems that they had been looking for a house to purchase for more that two and a half years. They were a young family with two adorable children. Although the husband had a good job, they kept being turned down for a bank loan. Every time they found the right house, they were turned down. They had become very despondent over this experience and had come to me in hopes of manifesting a solution. As with the previous couple, I told them both to imagine opening a letter containing the approved mortgage papers standing by their mailbox. These people actually came to my lecture that evening to show me the mortgage papers which were sitting in their mailbox when they arrived home from my office. The interesting thing is that the second couple was able to manifest more quickly than the first. There was less of a time lag between their desire and its physical manifestation. They won the Grace race.

Miracle Light

While I lived in India, I lectured almost every evening. One of my favorite groups that I spoke to was the Ramalinga Society of Chennai. I lectured to them every week. Swami Ramalinga, for whom the group was named, was one of the most famous Gurus of the 1800's. Legend had it that he vanished into the light of God. I would often lecture to the group about God, light, and the nature of physical manifestation. Hundreds would come to the lectures which were held at this lovely old temple on the outskirts of town. I often joked that the reason they came to my lectures was to get the free meal that was served when I finished speaking.

One night, while I was lecturing, people in the crowd began to stand up and point at me. There was a big stir and finally the head of the Society came up and spoke to me. He told me that my body had become encased in a bright white light and that it was a sign from Swami Ramalinga. The crowd then came up to me one by one for a blessing. They believed that I was a channel for their beloved Swami. In the end, the members of the Society presented me a ceremonial shawl and pronounced me an honorary member.

What actually happened? My feeling is that Grace can express herself in an infinite number of ways. There are no limits. Hundreds of people witnessed this event. It was not my event. Grace was expressing herself to herself. Whether I was the spectacle or the spectator was unimportant. In retrospect, it would have been more interesting to watch it rather than to be watched. The danger in being watched is that you think they are watching you. You believe it is your power that they are watching and that they are empowering you. It is an "identity" crisis. The crisis ends with the realization that no "identity" ever existed. Grace has no identity. Grace just happens.

Miracle Light II

As I have mentioned in the introduction, I have healed and transmitted Grace to literally thousands of people. One encounter stands out in my mind, though, and I have shared it with only a few close friends. It all started one hot February morning in my office in Chennai. I was entertaining some guests from the U. S. The two ladies involved were both professional people. One was a Veterinarian from L. A. and the other lived in the San Francisco Bay area and ran a successful Advertising agency. We were discussing many different aspects of spirituality and its relationship to healing. In the course of the conversation, I asked them if they would be interested in experiencing the transmission of healing Grace directly. I suggested it because then they would be able to observe the effects first hand. They agreed and I began to work with them one at a time. The most powerful technique I use for the transmission of Grace is to transmit it directly through the eyes. After all, the eyes are the mirrors of the Soul. I basically looked into their eyes with my eyes. That's it. It is very powerful. The ladies both noticed that my face and body began to turn golden and very bright as they continued to stare into my eyes. In time, my body was gone and just the light remained. The interesting thing is that the ladies witnessed my body disappear and then reappear perhaps ten times over the course of an hour. The two professional ladies were blown away. They could not take their eyes off of mine. The ladies both felt that they had witnessed a true miracle and they said that they could never again doubt the existence of God.

What happened? I don't know. It had never happened to me before. Although I was surprised, I knew that I was not the owner of the experience, because, as I have said over and over again, Grace can express herself, in any way, at any time.

Miracle Birth

I want to tell you the story of a miracle. But first I want to explain what led up to it so that you can understand what makes it so special. It all started in late 2005. My son Joshua, the oldest of my five children, was living in Arizona at the time. On October 18th, 2005, Josh unexpectedly died in his sleep. His liver had failed. Our family was crushed.

Shortly after this event, I began receiving Oneness Blessings. I went on to attend the August, 2006, 21 Day Process, in India, with my "life partner" Irene. Irene and her family are important to this story as well. You see, Irene's daughter, had recently become pregnant with her first child. On Tuesday morning, January 30, 2007, she gave birth to a little girl at 5:32 PST. Now here is the interesting thing. Josh, my son who died, was also born on January 30th. He was born at 5:31 PST. They were born one minute apart and birth times are accurate to plus or minus one minute. They were born 35 years to the minute, apart.

Let's think about this. There are 1440 minutes in a day and 365 days in a year. This means that there are 525000 minutes in a year. So the chances of any two people being born on the same day and at the same minute are 525000 x 525000 or about 1 in 27 billion. And the chances of someone in your extended family being born at the exact same moment as another individual in your family are simply incalculable.

What is significant to me about this event is that it shows again how Divine Grace can operate in such awesome harmony and such perfect synchrony.

Miracle Awakening

I was often asked by my teacher to initiate high officials in the Indian government into extremely powerful Siddha Meditation techniques. These techniques were not commonly available and it was always a great pleasure for me to impart them. One evening, an official from the Tamil Nadu State Police came for initiation. I remember that I instructed him in the Shiva Shuksha Mantra technique which was said to tremendously accelerate personal spiritual development. The initiation went smoothly and the young officer was very pleased with the calmness and increased awareness that he was experiencing. We parted company that evening and I asked him to return the next evening so that I could meditate again with him. I wanted to make sure that he was using the technique correctly and that he continued to experience benefits from the practice.

Early the following morning, I received a rather frantic call from the young officer. It seems that shortly after he had gone to sleep that previous evening, he heard a tremendous explosion go off inside his head. Brilliant colors began to appear and he began to see his charkas (energy centers) spinning inside of him. He said that he was hearing the sound of mantras being chanted and that he saw visions of Hindu Gods all around him. He told me that when he looked up all he could see were heavenly angels praying to him. He was clearly frightened by the experience. He said that he felt that he had become an enormous silent observer of everything. He then asked me if he should go to a hospital emergency room as he thought he had gone mad.

I replied to him the following statement. I said, "Sanjay, You are experiencing a Divine moment. It is the most important moment you will ever experience. Allow it to be. God has bestowed Divine Grace upon you and has Awakend you to God realization. You are now experiencing what the saints from the ancient times have described as the ultimate goal of human life. It is time to enjoy. It is time to celebrate." He asked me if he should still go to work. I said, "You will be much better at your job now because you will know what needs to be known. Now you can be of real service to your family, your fellow workers and to everyone you will ever meet. They will all be touched by your Presence". Finally, he asked me if he had to leave his family now as there was a tradition in India that the Awakened must leave everyday life and go off to the mountains to meditate. I asked him if he wanted to do this. He answered with an emphatic "No" and then went on to tell me how much he loved his wife and son. I told him not to worry. I let him know that God would always guide him into right action. I told him that he would forever be the embodiment of spontaneous right action. He expressed immediate relief and over the next few weeks his experience became integrated into his everyday life. His experience has been validated by numerous Saints as an authentic Awakening. The saints referred to him as a spontaneous Jivan Mukti.

Here is an interesting detail. Sanjay had never practiced any form of meditation or other spiritual practice. He had come to his initiation with a clean slate. He had no notions of what would happen. He was "innocent like a child". These are the ones who are most ripe for the descent of Grace. Sanjay became my best friend while I lived in India. We meditated many, many times together. I spent innumerable evenings with his lovely family. It is my hope that by sharing this precious experience with the world, I am letting him know just how deeply I appreciated being a spectator to his Awakening.

"The Buddha in the form of a child"

It all began in September of 2000 when I had what, in India, was called a Nadi leaf reading. The Nadis were predictions for your present life etched on palm leaves. They were usually in the ancient Tamil language and written in the form of poetry . The predictions were said to be made by Gurus, hundreds or even thousands of years ago. They were said to be the Gurus' predictions for you in this lifetime. A trained "Nadi Reader", would translate the poetry into modern Tamil and then the modern Tamil would be translated into English. My particular Nadi was from the famous Agustya Nadis, said to be from the great Indian Yogi, Agustya, one of the authors of the Vedas.

I found my Nadi to be very interesting but, over time, I had forgotten all about it. A couple of years later, I was sitting having lunch with a spiritual teacher of mine and I happened to mention the Nadi. He asked to see a copy of it so I gave it to him to read. Some days later, the holy man and I were again sitting and talking when, suddenly, out of the blue, he looked up at me and asked, "Have you met the Buddha in the form of a child yet"? He was attempting to authenticate the Nadi by verifying that a certain prediction actually took place during the correct time period. At first, I didn't even know what he was talking about. Then, I realized that he was referring to a prediction in my Nadi which stated that in September, 2002, I would meet the Buddha in the form of a child and that I would perform service to him. I remember that moment vividly. I broke into a cold sweat. I answered him "Yes", though, up until that moment, I did not even realize that the prediction had actually come true.

Here is the story behind it. One day, in the course of my work, I visited the office of a professional person in Southern

California. I am being intentionally vague in order to protect the privacy of those involved. We were engaged in a rather spirited conversation when a framed photograph on a table caught my eye. I went over to take a closer look. The photo contained a number of saffron robed monks encircling a little blond haired boy. I could not take my eyes off of it and finally I asked, "Kate, What is this picture about? What's going on and who is the little boy?" She answered that it was her five year old son, Jay and she proceeded to tell me the story of the picture.

She said that, one afternoon, a few months back, she heard a knock at the door of her home. She opened the door only to find a group of smiling Tibetan Buddhist monks looking at her with great anticipation. They introduced themselves and said that they had traveled all the way from Tibet. Then, they asked her some very specific questions. First, they asked if she had a son who was born at a very specific moment and location. She answered," yes". Then they asked her if they would be allowed to meet the little boy and ask him a couple of questions. She told me that she was so shocked by the whole thing that she could barely answer them. But something told her that this was an important moment. So she invited the monks into her living room and called her son Jay in. The monks unfolded some items which were wrapped in a brown cloth and then asked Jay to identify them. He grabbed three or four common items like glasses, a pipe and a cane and said, "I've been looking for these and proceeded to walk off into the bedroom with them". The monks seemed very excited. The monks then told Kate that Jay was the reason that they traveled all of this way. They went on to tell her that they believed that he was the reincarnation of the beloved head Abbot of their monastery in Tibet. As he was dying, the Abbot had asked his monks to search for him in his next incarnation in order to remind him who he was. They said that the high Tibetan astrologer had identified Jay's birth time and place as the Abbot's new incarnation. Finally, the monks asked Kate and her husband if they could visit Jay on a regular basis and perhaps teach him a little of the Tibetan language. The parents reluctantly agreed and the Tibetan monks left.

A month later, there was another knock at the door. This time it was a group of Chinese Buddhist monks. It seems that their astrology had also indicated that a person at the same date, time and place as Jay was the reincarnation of "the Buddha". The same type of verification procedure took place and the monks left satisfied that they had located the "Awakened One". The interesting thing is that the Chinese Buddhists did not know about the Tibetans Buddhist monks who had preceded them. The two groups had located Jay independently of each other!

Three months later, yes, there was another knock at the door. It was a group of Native Americans from Arizona. It seems that their Elders had a secret text that also predicted the date, time and place of a great holy person. Kate told me that she and Jay had just recently participated in a private ceremony for Jay held on the Arizona reservation.

So, let's review this story. My Indian Nadi predicted that I would meet the Buddha in the form of a child in Sept 2002. The Indian prediction came true. At the same time, the Tibetan Buddhist astrologer predicted Jay as the Buddhist Abbot. The Tibetan prediction came true. At the same time, the Chinese Buddhist astrologer predicted Jay as the Buddha. The Chinese prediction came true. And finally, at the same time, the Native American elders predicted Jay as a God-man. Their prediction also came true. Now ask yourself how four different, divergent cultures could be driven to locate a single individual in yet a fifth culture all at the same time. This is not something out of the movies. This actually happened and there were many who know of this event.

My fondest memory was the morning that Jay and I sat on

the couch together, milk and cookies in hand, and watched "Spongebob Squarepants" on the television. I realized, at that moment, that though this Buddha child may some day have a tremendous impact on the human race, he was still a little boy who just loved being who he was. Jay was a California Buddha. This Buddha loved to play soccer. This Buddha was good with video games. This Buddha will probably date and perhaps get married and have his own "Little Buddhas". It is important that we understand that Jay, the Buddha incarnation, chose these circumstances for a reason. The Divine wanted him in this spot, at this time, for a very specific reason. It must have been a pretty important reason because the representatives of four different cultures were sent to locate him. To me, it is reminiscent of the story of the three wise men, who followed that star to Bethlehem, more than 2000 years ago, in order to locate the Christ child.

This story is yet another indication that all things, in all places, operate in perfect harmony with each other and that, through the power of Divine Grace; circumstances can combine in such a way so that one's entire life becomes a miracle.

My Awakening

In the Summer of 2004, I had just returned from two years of teaching and healing in India. I was completely exhausted and malnourished and I was so happy to be home again in Southern California. I remember that I just wanted to sit at the beach every day and have lots of pizza, french fries and cherry soda.

One day, I happened to read in the newspaper that Sri Amritanandamayi, "the famous hugging Saint", was going to be in Los Angeles for a public appearance. Though I admired her tireless efforts to transform the suffering of the world, I was feeling "burnt out" on Gurus, so I was reluctant to go see her.

At the last minute, I chose to go to see "Ammachi" in L.A. As I entered the great hall where she was meeting people, something came over me and I made a deeply conscious commitment to again seek Enlightenment. The hall where she was giving individual blessing was jam packed. There were literally thousands waiting for her Cosmic hug. In the wee hours of the morning, it was finally my turn. She lovingly held me and whispered mantras in my ear for what seemed like the longest time. Finally, she released me from her Divine arms, and I turned to weave my way back through the crowds. All of the sudden, Ammachi rose up out of her chair, physically reached over several people and grabbed me by the arm. She pulled me back so that we were again face to face and she said in perfect English, "Are you sure that you want it?" I knew exactly what she meant. I knew she was asking me if I was truly ready for Enlightenment. She was letting me know, in no uncertain terms, that it was my time and she was giving me one last chance to back out. I quickly answered "yes" and she shook her head approvingly and smiled.

I got to bed around 4 AM with my head still reeling from what had taken place. I had just fallen into a deep sleep when, all of the sudden, I heard the sound of an explosion that was so loud that I immediately thought the house I lived in had just blown up. The top of my head felt like it was gone as well and I definitely thought that I was dead. Slowly, I came back into the body and found that the house and I were still in tact. But something had changed. My whole world view, my consciousness, had gone through a dramatic shift and for the first time in my life, I felt Awake. I felt awakened to my true identity. I felt infinite and I knew, beyond the shadow of a doubt, that my life would never be the same again. Also, Ammachi left two words that kept going round and round, like a mantra, inside my head. They were the two words American Buddha. I am certain that Ammachi created the initial impulse for American Buddha and as you will soon see, Amma and Bhagwan then went on to manifest it.

My Enlightenment

Now, I want to share with you my last miracle story. It is a story that will, without question, happen to each and every one of you some day. Although it is the story of final Awakening, an Awakening to Oneness or to Unity Consciousness, it is actually a story which took lifetimes of experiences to create. The fact that I survived it all to get to the final Awakening is a miracle in itself.

I was in India at the time. I was at the Golden City in the State of Andrea Pradesh. I remember that it was a very hot, humid morning in late April. I was with a group of perhaps 40 westerners and we were all waiting to meet with Archarya Samadarshini. She is one the three principle disciples of Amma and Bhagwan, the reknown Avatars who have millions of followers throughout the world. Samadarshini is said to exist in a rather unique state of consciousness. It is said the she is at the level of development equivalent to a Christ or a Buddha. To meet her is to meet love in human form. There is no other way that I can describe it.

When she walked into the large meeting hall that we had gathered in, the air immediately became charged with a sense of uncontainable joy. She was a young woman, perhaps in her early thirties, dressed in pure white monk's attire. Her eyes were stunning. They were an endlessly deep dark brown. She sat on a chair before us and motioned us to come up very close to her. We all quickly surrounded the chair and giggled. As soon as she spoke, I could tell that she was very sharp. This was a very intelligent individual. But it was her compassion that was completely and utterly overpowering. It was as if she selected each of her words for the perfect transmission of Divine Love. She asked us to speak one at a time. She wanted to know our story. As we each spoke, it was clear that she was replying directly to our Souls. Each of our stories were different. Life had guided each one of us through a difficult and circuitous route that ended at this moment, at this spot, in her Divine Presence.

Finally, the microphone was handed to me. I remember it so clearly. I reached to my right and gripped the microphone with my hand. But something seemed very different. My hand appeared not to be my personal hand anymore. I looked up into the stunning eyes of the saint and I began to speak. I recall giving my name and where I was from in the states. Then these words seemed to exit my mouth from an unfathomable source as if the Divine had suddenly taken me over. I said, "May I ask you favor? She answered "Yes" in a soft tone. I said the following," I want to thank Amma and Bhagwan, personally, for Awakening me to Oneness. Would you thank them for me right now?" Samadarshini proceeded to close her eyes. For more than ten minutes, there was the most intense silence imaginable. I sat transfixed through it all. I heard crying. Many in our group of westerners were in tears as it was a deeply moving experience for everyone present. Finally, the young saint opened her eyes. She looked directly into my eyes and said the following," You have your Oneness. Amma and Bhagwan have blessed you with Oneness and you will be directed by Divine Grace for the rest of your life. From this moment onward, Bhagwan is the doing. You are just the witness."

And with those simple words, my destiny changed. It

completely changed. There was so much support for my activities after that. My book, this book, American Buddha, immediately was approved for publication. An audio and video series manifested out of nowhere. Seminars seemed to manifest out of thin air. People from all over the world started e-mailing or contacting me by phone asking for healing or to become my student. Everywhere I go, now, there is invariably a request for a healing or a blessing. Even my bank teller asked me for a blessing this morning. It is a far cry from just a few months back when I had all but given up on the book project. The book, American Buddha, and my life have become a miracle. Divine Grace has descended upon me and I am forever a vehicle for the Creator. I am that Oneness and my only wish is for you to also become that Oneness.

Now, you may ask what the difference is between Awakening and the state of Oneness or Unity Consciousness. I would put it this way. Awakening is a personal Enlightenment. You are Enlightened, but your world remains a divided world. In the state of Oneness or Unity, the divisions disappear and there is no more separation between you and your world. There is no more distinction between the personal and the universal. The Universe simply becomes an aspect of your personal self. Therefore, the real power to transform the world exists only in the state of Oneness.

Chapter 2
ANSWERS

What if one day your dreams became your reality? What if one day, all of the parts of your life suddenly fit together; perfectly? What if, instead of struggling, life began to push you along? What if synchronicity became ordinary living and the right circumstances seemed to manifest out of nowhere? What if you could know and do anything? What if the normal laws of cause and effect seem not to apply to you anymore? What if good things just kept happening to you in rapid succession? And what if this was happening to you without the slightest effort? That is the experience of Oneness.

If this is your present experience, then know full well that it is no accident. You should know that the life of the Divine is now pouring through you and that you have become one with the process of creation. You should know that the "small you", has unknowingly dissolved into the Cosmic you. Just know that you are no longer the dreamer. You have become the dream. Your destiny is now a Divine destiny and you are forever at peace with it all because you perceive that there is only Divine Oneness everywhere and this Oneness flows through all things. Divine Oneness is pure experience. You are this Oneness. You are all there ever was, is, or will be. You are the birds in the sky. You are this beautiful ocean. You are love. You are light. You cannot be located. You cannot be quantified. You cannot be defined in any way because, you are only Oneness. Oneness is an actual experience that can be lived in contemporary life. Oneness is my sole reason for existing. I am here to step up to the plate and say, "Yes, I am this. You are this. This is this. You should live this. This alone is real. Normal people can experience Oneness and you can too". The following questions and answers are designed to give you, the reader, a deep insight into the experience of the Awakened consciousness. Through these questions and answers, you too will begin to vibrate with an Awakened consciousness.

Q) What is the nature of Awakening?

A) Awakening is not an object of experience. This is why the Buddha would never describe his experience. Awakening is not a mental process. It is something other than mind. It is indescribable simply because if I told you what it was, you wouldn't believe me. Though there are no words, it is very real and one is very moved by the experience.

Q) What is the nature of Grace?

A) Grace is the catalyst. It is the sole cause for Awakening. No real growth can occur without it. Awakening is just another name for a permanent state of Grace. As a child depends on its mother, so do the Awakened depend on Grace.

Q) Is this moment a dream?

A) Yes. It is a very good question. This is all a dream. I swear that you are dreaming and that every moment is just another dream. You have created them all and none of them are real. This is a movie. All of these lives that you have lived, millions of them, are just dream sequences. They will go on forever. Your soul is the silent witness of your dreams. Take refuge in the fact that the dream and the dreamer have the same source. Just as the soap bubble is just soap, the dream and the dreamer are just the One.

Q) I have heard that an Awakened person does not experience suffering. Is this true?

A) Yes, there is no suffering, but this is too simplistic. Suffering infers a mental process. Awakening is not mental. Awakening is not emotional, physical or even spiritual. It is beyond these things and is not subject to anything. It is not a thing. There is no way to tell an Awakened individual from an ignorant one. There are no clues. There are no tests. Yes, there is no suffering, but only in the sense that there is no connection anymore. An Awaken One's point of view will be the only a difference. What's the difference? An Awakened One just experiences. There is no interpretation. They will experience what you experience only they will experience it completely. There is freedom of choice. If an Awakened One puts their hand in a fire, they might scream or they might not. But the PAIN will be exactly the same. It will be just as real. The difference is that while the pain will be felt, the suffering will not. Suffering is just a mental process associated with the interpretation of pain.

Q) What is the relationship of silence to Awakening?

A) There is single energy, and its nature is silence. The more silent we are, the more powerful our personal energy will become. One day, you will become perfectly still and in that perfect stillness you with vanish into Oneness. At that point, you will become one with all things. You will know the knower. You will become a co-creator. You will no longer experience boundaries because the boundaries will also be you. It all will be you and there will be no such thing as the not-you. You will be living the mind of God. There will be nowhere to go. There will be nothing to do. You will be content. You will be the context. You will be Awakened to Oneness.

Q) What is the value of work?

A) All play and no work keeps you in bondage. Work infuses Grace into life.

Q) Who am I?

A) There are three powers that interact in nature. They are creation, maintenance and destruction. You are just the self-interacting dynamics of these three powers. There actually is no you. You are never, ever acting. You have never been involved. There are just the three powers interacting upon themselves eternally.

Q) Who am I?

A) You are God's favorite child.

Q) Who are you?

A) I express the light of God. To the extent that you interact with me, your life will be transformed accordingly. This process is completely automatic. I do not participate in it. Why? To my experience, there is no me and there is no you. The Oneness exists as pure experience. The concept of subject and object is now seen as an experiential misinterpretation. They are, in truth, interchangeable. Our brains tend to fragment our reality. I am not denying the differences. A rock is not a chair. Only, the rock and the chair and everything that used to be the not-me are now seen in the light of a singular experience. This singular experience has its own identity and purpose. The personal "I" is experienced as one of an infinite number of expressions of this singular intelligence. I call this experience Oneness.

Q) What can I do to grow closer to God?

A) You can do nothing. God must grow closer to you. It is her choice. She will find you. She already has. She will infuse you with Divine Grace. That is the key to growing closer to God.

Q) What is the value of silence?

A) People believe that silence is boring and empty. They run and think and then run and think some more. A yogi experiences the truth. He knows that action is darkness and that silence is light. He knows that action is empty while silence is full. He knows that silence is the basis of all activity. Silence is ever-full, flawless and unchanging. The yogi knows the secret.

Q) Are you a Guru?

A) No! I am. I am experience. I am Grace. I am God. You are God too. I have no philosophy and espouse no particular tradition. I teach Oneness. I teach what I am.

Q) What is more important, Awakening or manifestation?

A) Both are important. Both must be addressed. They are like two sides of a coin. You need to be Awakened because without it, living is a waste. Awakening is just another name for happiness. You also have a body and you need to make it comfortable. If you watch your thoughts for a while, you will notice that ninety-five percent of them are about survival. You need not to have to worry about your rent, your next meal, you health or your boy or girlfriend. Find the balance. Work hard and seek Divine Grace.

Q) What is the purpose of life?

A) The purpose of life is to play and play and play until you get tired. Then you can go home and rest.

Q) Would you speak to us about Oneness?

A) Oneness is Self-evident. It is a Self-illuminated, Self-referral truth. Oneness can never be the product of equivocation. Oneness is not open to conjecture. The actual process of analyzing the Oneness cannot be separated from the Oneness itself. The three dimensional reality that we live in, in reality, is just One, One, One. And it is experienced. Oneness is a direct experience. Trying to understand it, intellectually, is not of valuable. Understanding Oneness is directly opposed to experiencing Oneness.

Q) How should we live our lives? Do you have any advice?

A) Seek Grace by getting Oneness Blessings regularly. Nothing else is important. There is no need to push or pull anymore. You have done the hard work before this life and it is time for you to sit back and relax. Leave the driving to God. So, I am not asking you to stop or start anything. You can't get rid of your bad habits but you can watch them. Watching them in the Grace will gradually weaken them. Life is Self-propelled, that is, it goes by itself. Nature is the doer and we are not actually in control of what is our experience. If you can just understand that we are only here to experience rather than to be in control of our experience, you are miles ahead.

Q) What is the relationship of mind to our manifestations?

A) Your "personal mind" is the great fragmenter in the sense that it is constantly dividing the Oneness of life. Your mind can become a useful tool for manifestation as soon as you see that you are not your mind. Otherwise, if you identify with the mind as your "personal mind", then each fragment of this unreal mind will create a doubt. And each doubt you have about your manifestation in your "personal mind" will continue to divide and weaken the power of your manifestation. Each division will present a barrier to your manifestation. A yogi manifests effortlessly because he or she experiences no localized mind and he/she experiences no sense of fragmentation or doubt because the doubter cannot be located. A yogi knows that all manifestation takes place in the non-local mind because it alone is real. When you learn to manifest from the non-local mind, you will manifest with the power of the Oneness.

Q) How does destiny play into spiritual development?

A) We all have a destiny. If you are very still, you can feel it. Destiny is that circle of thoughts surrounding us. It is our rut. Destiny is a predictable sequence of thoughts which leads to the same sequence of actions which produce the same consequences. Destiny is Divine Law. It is fixed and it is our ultimate addiction.

Q) What is Love?

A) I find solace in the fact that love exists. I am truly in love with everyone I meet. I can't help it. Even the unpleasant ones move me deeply. My heart is hopelessly hooked on humans. Their eyes speak volumes to me. They are my Soul's support. I melt and die in love for them. I vanish in love. I bow to love completely.

Q) Who is God?

A) God is the light of Love. God permeates life through Love. God is Grace. There is no not-God. God is Personified Love. God greases the wheels of Life. God puts the spring in Spring.

Q) Speak to us about spiritual paths. Why are there so many?

A) There are many paths but only one goal. The diversity of the paths is the result of the variations in language, cultural specific norms, religion, climate, etc. Though the goal is hard wired into every human nervous system on earth, the paths are soft wired and flexible. The paths change with the fluid nature of space/time. The paths are also influences by planetary placement and other solar events.

Q) How do relationships work?

A) Humans are like a puzzle with some of the pieces missing. Most of us spend our lives looking for the missing pieces through relationships. We are attracted to what is missing in ourselves. That is the cause of attraction. We fill the missing parts in ourselves with those of our beloved.

Q) What is the universal language, the universal system, the universal technique for Awakening?

A) It is the Oneness Blessing. Oneness Blessing provides the missing component. Oneness Blessing provides Divine Grace. When there is enough Grace, you Awaken. When the Grace of Oneness Blessing transforms your biochemistry, you Awaken. Oneness Blessing fills your nerves and receptor sites with a strong, coherent, pure bioelectric signal. Impurities are burnt away by the strength of this Divine current. The chemicals in the synaptic cleft are transformed by the Grace signal. As impurities dissolve, the conductivity of the Grace increases until the central nervous system is then able to sustain a much greater Grace signal. Eventually, the ultrastrong Grace signal permeates waking, dreaming, and sleeping consciousness and your Brain "Awakens". It is a sort of a biochemical sunrise.

Q) Do I have control of my life?

A) It is only by God's infinite Grace and Compassion that you even have your next breath. You are knowingly or unknowingly a Divine vehicle. Awaken! Then the Divine can take your hand and lead you back home.

Q) Who are you?

A) I am not who you think I am because you are not who you think you are. When you become who you are then you will know who I am.

Q) What is the relationship of karma to manifestation?

A) Manifestation is simply attention. What we attend to is what our reality will become. What we attend to creates our future karma. What we attend to is what attracts us because we are attracted to what we need to work on in this life. What we attend to will also be what is attracted to us. We are attracted to our karma. It is the ultimate Law of Attraction, "Like attracts like". So we will find it easiest to manifest our karma. If it is not our karma to manifest a certain thing, it will be almost impossible to manifest it. A lot of karma will happen to us to manifest something that which is not in our karmic path. It is Natural Law and it can't be avoided. Remember, all of the rest of creation is affected by our manifestations so if creation doesn't want it, then it will put up intense resistance.

Q) What is right action? How can we judge right from wrong?

A) It is not so much how you act as where you are acting from. For now, I would suggest that you adhere to socially agreed upon norms.

Q) Can an Awakened person make a mistake?

A) Yes and No. An Awakened person can make a logical error but their experience of Oneness would remain untainted by any action.

Q) Can a yogi act effectively in the "real" world?

A) Yogis are the ultimate efficiency experts. Every thought and resulting action of a yogi has an immensely powerful effect at an absolute minimum of energy. Therefore, a yogi will be the most grounded, practical, "real" person that you will ever meet.

Q) Who am I? Am I really this body? Am I really this mind? Or am I just the Soul?

A) There is only one body, and it is a universal body. There is only one living being in creation and it is creation herself. There is only one consciousness and she has expressed herself in an infinite number of forms. Suffering comes from identification with these various forms. We are not a localized body. We are an infinite body. You and I are not you and I. We are both an aspect of one infinite living being. This being is ALIVE! Its nature is Oneness. In this Oneness, there is absolute freedom. In this Oneness, there is absolute bondage. In this Oneness, there is no more you, so there is complete freedom. There is liberation. In this Oneness, there is complete bondage. This is because, in this Oneness, you are bound to act on behalf of the universal you. In this Oneness, there is complete love. Everyone and everything is as near and dear to you as your own self. It is all your body. If the earth is your body then how could you continue to damage her? If the other people in the world are actually you, then how could you possibly hurt anyone anymore?

Q) Would you talk to us about Oneness?

A) In Oneness, the observer, observed, and the process of observation are indistinguishable from one other. In Oneness, they are a completely interchangeable experience. In Oneness, you do not know if you are looking at a wall or whether the wall is looking at you. This is because Oneness is the sum total of experience. It is all sides from all angles. It is almost absurd to take a side on an issue because you also see that the opposing side is equally you. It is all you, only the "personal you" does not exist anymore. You have become Oneness. You are now the Universe. You are now the goal of existence. You are finally at home.

Q) What is the highest truth?

A) The highest truth is that what is, simply is. But what most of us live is that, what is, simply isn't. What is, can't be what it is. We won't allow it. We're in control. We will fight what is tooth and nail. We will employ specialists to help us change what is into what isn't. We'll get an army and go to war with what is. Then, when we win over what is, we will elect a leader who will change what is into what isn't. Then what is will be the right is.

Q) How do mantras work?

A) To understand mantras, you have to first understand the makeup of the mind. The mind is made up of language and language is based on words. Words, in turn, are made up of sounds. So, really, the mind is just a bunch of sounds. Mantras are sounds which organize the sounds of the mind. The theory behind the mantras is that if we can change the sounds that make up the mind, then we can change our lives.

Q) How should we live in this world?

A) Be practical. Be grounded. You have to live this world fully. The truth is that you can't become God unless you know her creation first.

Q) Please give us the experience of Oneness?

A) Close your eyes and sit quietly. Relax. Now allow these words to enter you:

I invoke the Presence

Now put your attention on the crown of your head.

Picture a golden ball of light just above the crown.

This golden ball of light is filled with Divine Grace.

Now, imagine the palms of my hands lying on the crown of your head.

Feel the Grace entering your crown area and then pouring through your entire body.

You are now filled with Divine Grace.

Feel yourself in all directions, both near and far.

You are omniscient, omnipresent, omnipotent, and all-pervading.

You are existence. This is all your own creation.

In waking, dreaming, and sleeping, you are only Oneness.

You are supportless....You are eternal.....You are silent......

Now, sit for 5 minutes in this Divine Grace. Let it integrate throughout your nervous system.

Q) Would you teach us techniques for Awakening as well as one for manifestation?

A) I can teach you very powerful techniques for Awakening, but they will make you poor. I can teach you very powerful wealth creating techniques, but they will tend to make you forget about God. Or I can transmit Divine Grace and give you all that you ever desired. It's your choice.

Q) What is the "Giving Light" technique?

A) Giving light is the oldest form of Grace Transmission. One sits in front of the teacher. The teacher gazes lovingly into your eyes. You become entrained to the teachers' consciousness. There is a non-verbal transmission of energy, of consciousness. His silent eyes can look deeply. Everything becomes available to him. Deep rooted karmas are uprooted and dissolved instantly. The student is saved great suffering. The technique is completely effortless. Both teacher and student must participate for it to work. Openness is the key.

Q) How can I quickly connect to the universe?

A) There is a subtle variation of consciousness with each heartbeat. To know the heart is to know the universe. The heart is plugged right in. Touch the radial pulse of your wrist with the tips of your fingers. It is Natures' perfect feedback loop. Become the pulse to become God.

Q) What are the best points of entry for Healing Grace?

A) The points of entry are the eyes, the heart, the right palm placed below the navel and the radial pulse. The eyes contain the knowledge of the Soul. The navel contains the knowledge of the body and the past lives. The pulse contains the knowledge of the constitution and feelings. The heart contains the emotional core. Please be careful of heart healing. It can be a volatile area to work on.

Q) How do you prevent the mind from being distracted?

A) The mind IS distraction. It will go on like this forever. Just love your mind the way you love your dear old grandmother who talks a lot. You are the Soul. You will go on like this forever. You can never be distracted.

Q) Can anyone benefit from repeating mantras that are picked out of a book?

A) No! Mantras are like seeds. Gurus are like farmers. Gurus know the right seasons, the fertilizers, and the right seeds to produce the greatest harvest.

Q) Can karma ever come to an end?

A) Karma is action. Soul is inaction. They are both eternal.

Q) My mind remains clear for a day or two and then turns dull for a couple of days. What causes this?

A) Mind is in the field of action. The field of action is the field of the Three Gunas (creation, maintenance, and destruction). The field of action is the field of change. Mind is constantly changing between the three. In the creation or Sattva phase, mind is clear. In the maintenance or Rajas phase, there is clarity but it is in a state of movement. It does not feel as clear. In the destruction or Tamas phase, mind has moved into dullness. These three phases revolve eternally. Even after Awakening, they are there. Only the Awakened are disengaged from the effects of action.

Q) What is the heart?

A) Heart is the physical seat of the Soul.

Q) Who am I?

A) The answer to your question is that it can't be answered. Your question is the source of all of your suffering. You think you are this or that thing. You think that you need to be defined. You are indescribable.

Q) Why was I born?

A) You were never born. You are and have always been eternal, non-changing bliss. The delusional mind/ body/ personality appears to exist then not exist. But like a mirage, it was never real to begin with.

Q) What is it that leaves the body?

A) Soul is the only reality. The body is the superimposition. The body drop away from the eternal Soul.

Q) What is the significance of Dharma?

A) Dharma is your personal map home. What is simply is. That is the working definition of Dharma.

Q) Is the world perceived even after self realization?

A) Yes. Only the perceiver perceives the world as it actually is.

Q) I am distracted during my meditation. What can I do?

A) I'm distracted too. I'm distracted all of the time. No matter what I see, no matter what I do, no matter what I think, only the Self is there. I can't seem to shake it. What can I do?

Q) Why is living the Truth limited to a few?

A) It should not be. This is changing now. A great transformation is about to occur. The human race is about to go through a spiritual awakening. This has never before happened. It is a blessing that you are alive to witness this event.

Q) What is the mind? Where does it come from?

A) Mind was originally created to serve the Soul on earth. Mind was an action tool. Mind acted with the body to fulfill the need of the moment. In Kali Yuga, the mind mistook itself for the Soul. Mind disconnected from its source and suffering on earth began.

Q) Whose mind is it? How do I control it?

A) Mind is not your mind. There is no you. There is a cosmic mind. It is a huge thought repository for all humans. Because it is not your mind, you can never control it.

Q) How do I realize God?

A) The real question you should ask yourself is how you got to the point where you believe that you are not already God.

Q) Is God the source of the ego?

A) Ask yourself if you are the source of your ego because you are God.

Q) How do I get released from my karma?

A) You are released as soon as you stop holding on to your karma. You are not your karma. It is just action interacting with itself. You don't exist.

Q) Does distance have any effect on Grace?

A) Distance is concept in the mind. Only mind is localized. Grace is not related to mind. Therefore, distance.

Therefore, distance is not an issue for Grace to overcome.

Q) What is the cause of suffering in the world?

A) You are the cause. You and suffering are one and the same. If you eliminate the you, then you automatically eliminate the suffering.

Q) What is the astral body?

A) The astral world is like a nite club that you can go to after hours and your astral body is like your evening attire.

Sometimes you wake up the next morning with a headache but you know you had a great time while you were there. Think of the astral experience as Gods' version of an XBOX 360 video game.

Q) If I don't have free will then whose will is it?

A) You are completely free to do exactly what God wants.

Q) Yoga means union. What is in union with what?

A) It's a great question. In theory, Yoga is the Self seeking Itself through Itself. Only, it is an illusion to believe that the Self would ever believe it is not the Self in the first place.

Q) Is the ego real?

A) It is real to who is asking the question. Only who is asking is not real.

Q) How do I know if action is mine or not?

A) If your sense of "mine' is infinite, then it is your action.

Q) Is the world within me or outside of me? Does it exist apart from me?

A) You are the Self. That is all that matters.

Q) Are there a heaven and a hell?

A) There are both heaven and hell. They exist until you realize that you made them up.

Q) Can we see God in concrete form?

A) Yes, An Avatar is localized God.

Q) Should I renounce the world to obtain liberation in this life?

A) Why would you renounce yourself in order to find yourself?

Q) What is more important in spiritual practice, the mind or the heart?

A) Heart is the seat of God. Heart is the source of the mind.

Q) How is Grace obtained?

A) Oneness Blessing is the easiest way.

Q) Can you help me get rid of my attachment to the world?

A) Get rid of the idea of you and me and, presto, you are not attatched.

Q) How do I realize the self?

A) It is already realized. You are already realized. That is all you have to realize.

Q) What is "turiya"?

A) Turiya is the Self as it is co-mingled with waking, dreaming, and sleeping.

Q) Does a Guru use occult powers to make us realize the self or is the mere power of their self-realization enough?

A) Occult powers are just glorified ignorance. Guru is Self-embodied. Guru needs nothing else.

Q) Can Awakening come and go?

A) It depends on your perspective. Yes, the Self can express itself and then become hidden again. But, no, you are already eternally Awakened so how can you come and go?

Q) Who is the Master? Who is the disciple?

A) They are both. They are neither. They co-exist. They create each other.

Q) What is the best time to meditate?

A) What time is it?

Q) Can we have more than one spiritual master?

A) Yes, you can have many but really there is just the One.

Q) How do books help with Self-realization?

A) They are good to sit on while you become Self-realized.

Q) How is restlessness removed from the mind?

A) First, you should realize that your mind is already removed from you. Your mind is not located within you so it is not your personal mind that is restless. The restlessness exists outside of you. It is happening within the universal mind field. The restlessness could be related to the weather, or an event in Ethiopia. It could even be from the thoughts of someone who has long since past. There could be an infinite number of sources. One thing is for sure, though, your restlessness is already removed from your mind.

Q) What is the nature of reality?

A) Nature is polarized Oneness. That is the reality. The nature of reality is that reality is just nature.

Q) You tell us that the "I" is an illusion. Who created this illusion?

A) There is no illusion. There is only the Self. That is the only reality. Live this because there is nothing else. Pray for Grace. Pray for God to wake you up. It is a waste of time to analyze it. It is not your mind. It is not your body. It is not your persona. You are just happening to yourself.

Q) What is happiness? Is it our real nature? Can happiness be permanent?

A) Happiness is the Self and the Self is permanent. So our true nature is only permanent happiness.

Q) Where and when do I exist?

A) First, you have to answer how and why you think you exist? When you can answer these two questions, then where and when will be made clear to you.

Q) How can I know the real I from the false I?

A) They are both false so what's the point.

Q) How do I realize that all of the world is God?

A) Who is asking the question? God is asking the question. If you are God, then all of your world will also be God.

Q) I know nothing. Does this mean that I am Awakened?

A) If you know nothing, then you know way too much to be Awakened.

Q) Can the world exist with no one to perceive it?

A) The world can't exist even with someone to perceive it.

Q) Does the world exist for others while I sleep?

A) There is no world. There are no others and it is time to wake up.

Q) Are you aware of yourself and your surrounding as much as I am?

A) I am aware of as much as I am. The only questions I have of you is who is your "I am"? Who the "yourself" that you attach to me and what are the "surroundings" that you are placing me in?

Q) What is the difference between meditation and distraction?

A) No difference. They both are a distraction.

Q) How do I reconcile work with spiritual practice?

A) What is not spiritual? Is it not all the Self? Are you not God? Work is Divine.

Q) Is there really a mind?

A) Yes, but it is not yours.

Q) Are thoughts matter?

A) Thoughts don't matter.

Q) Does spirit generate matter?

A) Spirit is matter. So matter was not generated. Matter co-exists as an expression of spirit.

Q) There are many methods and techniques. We all want to succeed in them. How can we overcome our impatience?

A) There is nothing to overcome. Impatience is just experience. It is part of the landscape you are living. It is not a good or bad thing.

Q) When I meditate, there is a feeling that I exist, I am present, I am aware. How can I have this dissolve into an egoless state of just awareness?

A) Why do you want an egoless meditative state in the first place? It may take your suffering away for awhile. But when you come out you will still be the same person as before. Nothing will have changed. So what's the point? You need to live this world. You were not born just to hide out inside your head. Live an Awakened existence. Then your entire life will become an egoless meditative state. To accomplish this, something other than you must intervene on your behalf. Grace must intervene and change you.

Q) How can I know that the spiritual search in which I am involved is not an ego trip? How can I know that it is an authentic religious search?

A) You can never know this because the "you" that is assessing the authenticity of your search is not authentic. "You" is the opposite of authentic. You can know the search is authentic only when Divine Grace finds you. The only authentic search is God's search for you.

Q) If the ego is unreal, does it mean that the memories in my brain cells are unreal?

A) The memories in your brain cells are real. The experiencer that you attribute these memories to is not real. They are not "your" memories. They are not "your" brain cells. These memories in the brain cells are impersonal. They are related to the universal process of experience.

Q) Is the process of spiritual transformation unreal?

A) It is completely unreal. The concept of spiritual transformation is the biggest roadblock to spiritual transformation. You already are as spiritual as you can ever be. So you can only transform yourself away from spirituality. Live what you are.

Q) Techniques, such as meditation, are shortcuts, but are

they not against the natural flow of nature?

A) Ignorance is against the natural flow of nature. A spiritual shortcut would hasten the elimination of ignorance. Therefore, shortcuts support the natural flow of nature.

Q) After millions and millions of years, one gets Awakened. But after millions and millions of years, another may not yet be Awakened. Why? What causes the difference?

A) God bestows Awakening in a seemingly random fashion. But it is not random. It is extremely precise. Just be aware that God has her own agenda. If you want to understand it better, I suggest that to realize that you are One with God.

Q) Is freedom opposed to surrender?

A) Freedom is a state of being and nothing in this life can interfere with this freedom. So nothing can ever be surrendered.

Q) Is self-actualization a basic need?

A) The Self alone exists. It has no needs. The ego has needs. It is never satisfied. The ego needs to become the Self. So the need is the basic need of the ego. Ego believes it can become the Self. Ego does not see that it is an overlay. Ego will vanish as the Self becomes aware of itself.

Q) How can mental processes help in achieving no-mind?

A) The mind can pray for Grace.

Q) Will you explain contemplation, concentration and meditation?

A) When I contemplate, I think about something. When I concentrate, I think only about something to the exclusion of all other things. And when I meditate, I forget about everything.

Q) What are some practical ways to develop the heart?

A) Serve others. Pray for Grace. Receive Oneness Blessings as often as possible. Heal your relationships.

Q) Buddha's asceticism seems opposed to the middle path. Please explain.

A) I don't agree with you. The Buddha's begging bowl was neither too big nor too small.

Q) Why is Samadhi-Cosmic Consciousness-called centering?

Q) Samadhi is the experience of being Self-Centered.

Q) Why is man insensitive?

A) Man believes that he is sensing from a central core. So he feels that he must protect himself from that which is outside of this core. He accomplishes this by limiting the amount of sense information he allows himself to experience in any given moment. The end result is that man senses very little. He is insensitive. The mistake is that there is no core to defend.

Q) Can love alone be enough for Awakening?

A) Yes. Love can manifest as an Awakening of the heart. But this is completely up to the Divine.

Q) Isn't it true that no method is powerful unless one is initiated into it?

A) Spiritual technology is useless unless it is transmitted properly.

Q) Isn't initiation and Grace of the master more important than techniques?

A) This is true. It is not so much the technique as it is the consciousness from whom it is imparted.

Q) How do we become capable of receiving?

A) First become capable of giving, giving, and giving! The rest will take care of itself.

Q) Should love be a continuous process?

A) Yes, it should be continuous but love is a blessing from the Divine. Your present love is conditional. It has peaks and troughs because it is associated with the core belief that you exist. Unconditional permanent love can exist only in a heart that has flowered through Divine Grace.

Q) When does love become devotion?

A) There is no difference.

Q) What is attachment? What is freedom?

A) There is only freedom. But, as soon as I say this, you will become attached to it.

Q) Can one be Awakened by bringing the body into a death-like state?

A) No! A death-like state can accompany a spontaneous Awakening.

Q) Should we consciously regulate our instincts?

A) That is ridiculous. Who is going to regulate them? It is your false sense of "you". "You", not your instincts, need to be regulated.

Q) How can we tell the false from the real in ourselves?

A) Ask yourself who is going to tell the false from the real. It is the one who answers who is false.

Q) Can you explain the process of mantra initiation? What is the reason for the secrecy of the mantras?

A) Initiation brings your mind to a place of receptivity. Mantra is transmitted from this point. It is like planting a seed. It must be planted in the best soil under optimal conditions. Mantras are structured in consciousness. Their power is known only to the teacher. Secrecy stems from teachers need to protect you from your own ignorance.

Q) What is the difference between indulgence and repression?

A) There is no difference. Both are the product of the same process. Both create tension. Both are unnatural. Both are extreme. Both create karma. Both create an emotional charge.

Q) What is the guru's role and significance in this world?

A) Guru is on the outside. Guru is free. Guru is God. Guru can help you to find your way out. That is her skill. Guru is not only Awakened. Guru is empowered to guide others to Awakening.

Q) What is the right attitude towards life?

A) What is simply is. Also, be very thankful to God for what is happening to you in this moment.

Q) What happens to polar opposites in the state of Oneness?

A) They are seen in the light of God. Then they lose their power to sway you anymore.

Q) Doesn't an immoral life create hindrances in meditation?

A) Yes, an immoral life makes the nervous system course and the experience in meditation less clear. But there is not a thing you can do about it other than to just be aware that it is happening and to pray for Divine Grace to transform it.

Q) Isn't it suppression to make an effort to avoid suppression or indulgence?

A) You can do nothing. You can't even do "nothing" because you will invariable try to indulge or suppress the "nothing". The only thing that you can do is to seek Grace through a Oneness Blessing. That's about it.

Q) Why has modern man become incapable of love?

A) You are implying that ancient man could love but he somehow lost that ability along the way. I agree. Modern man knows too much to love. He has lost his innocence. He has developed this propensity to think his world to death. He has squeezed every last drop of love out of his life. He has become dry and barren and alone as a result. Modern man comes to see me so that I can show him a way to think his way to love. I ruin his plan. I force him to experience this moment. I force him to experience that this moment IS love.

Q) What is your attitude toward handling the modern life of tensions and exertions?

A) Life is to be lived and you are God. You have enormous freedom to choose how to live it. Grace can help you find the middle path between rest and activity. Both are essential.

Q) What is normal and why is there so much pathology these days?

A) Awakening is normal. Everything else is pathological. Suffering is pathological because it is not an essential part to life. The human nervous system was never designed to suffer.

Something has happened. Man has become sick. Pathology is the absence of permanent happiness.

Q) Aren't all meditation techniques a form of "doing"?

A) Yes!

Q) Why do we continue to create suffering?

A) Suffering is all that we know. From birth our parents taught us to suffer. Society added to it by teaching us how to feel guilty if we didn't suffer. So when someone says to us that we could be happy all of the time, that happiness is our natural state we think that person is crazy. We think that they have a vested interest. Maybe they want our money. It's not our fault. It is all that we know. Trying to explain eternal happiness to anyone is like trying to explain dreaming to someone who has never dreamed.

Q) Can problems be solved through thinking?

A) What do you think? You will think yes or no or maybe or something in between. You certainly can find solutions using the mind. That is what the mind was originally intended for. Mind was a mechanism to get things done. Mind was the Soul's servant in this world. But the mind began to identify itself as the doer. This misunderstanding created a myriad of problems which the mind can't solve. Only Grace can intervene to set the whole thing straight again.

Q) Can science and religion meet?

A) Yes. It is all one thing. Matter and spirit are inextricably connected. Matter and spirit are expressions of the same source. They have already met. They just don't know it yet.

Q) Can you shed light on darkness?

A) Let me see?

Q) Is the process of transformation also a dream?

A) Yes! Transformation is completely illusory. I have often stated that the concept of transformation is the single greatest impediment to Self-realization.

Q) How do I know that the spiritual search is real?

A) It definitely isn't. Real is the searcher not the search.

Q) Why are we not Awakened?

A) You ARE Awakened.

Q) Can you define "non-doing"?

A) No. It cannot be defined in words. Non-doing transcends concepts. It is a state of being. Non-doing is structured in consciousness.

Q) Are there shortcuts to Awakening?

A) Oneness Blessing is the best shortcut I know of.

Q) Does the desire for Divinity have to be transcended?

A) Yes, it will have to go. But don't struggle with it. It is comforting to have while you are still in suffering.

Q) How do I include my enemy into my being?

A) Get rid of the concept of I and your enemy immediately disappears.

Q) How is the ego destroyed?

A) How can you destroy something that does not exist in the first place?

Q) Is it useful to remember the past or to know the future?

A) It is more useful to remember the future. Look! What am I doing? I am killing your logic. Over and over I am killing your logic to show you that you exist apart from your thoughts.

Q) When I meditate, I go beyond thought but there is still no happiness. What am I doing wrong?

A) You are having the thought of no happiness. If you were truly beyond thought, you couldn't entertain the thought of no happiness.

Q) Can you summarize your teachings?

A) You are God.

Q) How long will it take until my Self Realization?

A) As soon as you stop trying to realized your Self, you are Self Realized. Your Self is already Real. It is the only thing that is real in your life. Quit trying to make it more real.

Q) Is an intellectual understanding of the truth necessary?

A) No! Self Realization is so natural that many in it have no idea that they in it. That is because there is nothing to be in. Intellectual understanding simply helps to pacify the mind of the unrealized. The realized realize that they are not the intellect so intellectual understanding has no value to them.

Q) Is the experience of the highest Truth the same for everybody?

A) The experience is the same but it is expressed differently in each person.

Q) If we say, "Let thy will be done", then why do we need

to pray?

A) Prayer is Gods will. That's why we pray.

Q) Does God work her will through some chosen people?

A) We are all God's people. We are all equally important because there is nothing that is not Gods' work. You may be the shoe and I may be the lace but we are both necessary to tie the shoe.

Q) How do I keep my mind in order?

A) When you realize that you are not your mind, then you will be in order.

Q) How do I train my mind to think only good thoughts?

A) Why would you want to do that? What good would that do? You would suffer even more. There is no good thought. There is no bad thought either. Thoughts just exist. They have no intrinsic value and they are not even your thoughts. If they are not yours, then how would you be able to distinguish good from bad anyway? Thoughts are not good or bad. You are not good or bad. You are experience only. You are only the One.

Q) Is there one self or are there many selves?

A) Which self is asking the question? Which self is answering the question? Which self will think about the answer next week? Which self will come up with another question? Which self will die in the end? There is just One Self and it never needs to ask a question. This One Self will never die because it was never born in the first place. This Self is the One without a second.

Q) What is the significance of the Guru's Grace in the

attainment of liberation?

A) You cannot be liberated without the Guru's Grace!

Q) Can problems be solved through thinking?

A) Thinking IS the problem.

Q) There are many methods and techniques. We all want to succeed in them. How can we overcome our impatience?

A) There is nothing to overcome. Impatience is just experience. It is part of the landscape you are living. It is not a good or bad thing.

Q) What is the benefit in knowing that I am not my body?

A) Knowing it is of little importance. But experiencing that you are not your body is of critical importance. You must experience that you are not your body, mind, thoughts, or personalities. You are the Self. You are the One without a second. And only Divine Grace can create such an experience.

Q) You are here sitting in front of me and I am asking you a question. What is the basic difference between us?

A) The difference is that you believe that I am sitting in front of you. But I experience a fluid relationship where the roles of you and I are both interchangeable and co-created. I experience just one process interacting everywhere. My "I" sense permeates this interaction and this interaction permeates the "I" that you identify as mine. That is the only difference between our two experiences.

Q) What makes you so dispassionate?

A) I am content with the moment being just as it is. I need nothing. I am eternally fulfilled. That is why I am so passionate about this dispassionate state.

Q) What do you see?

A) I know that seeing is going on but there is no "I" sense to organize it. You are seen, of course. But the Self is the seer and also the seen.

Q) Is it love that provides the bridge between spirit and body?

A) Love is the body, the spirit, and the bridge between them.

Q) If the body disappears, does the knower disappear?

A) There are actually two knowers. One is the universal knower and the other is ego-based knower. The universal Self knows because there is nothing other than it to begin with. The universal Self as knower is non-local and will exist forever. It can never disappear. But the "I" sense of the ego-based knower will disappear with the body. The "I" sense is conjured up like a mirage in the desert.

Q) Is the witness permanent or not?

A) The Self is permanent. The witness is just the Self expressed through the body/mind.

Q) What is death?

A) Your life is death. What you are presently living is death. Death is not experiencing that everything, everywhere is filled with joy and bliss and happiness.

Q) What is this sense of a separate existence?

A) The sense of separation is due to a neurophysiologic defect which has developed over the course of time. Chemistry has created a gap in our experience. We feel estranged from a sense of wholeness. To use a metaphor, we have been thrown out of the Garden of Eden. Only Grace can transcend this gap. The Divine must intervene. Only the Divine is capable of rewiring the brain back to assume its original configuration.

Q) All teachers advise us to meditate. What is the purpose of meditation?

A) The purpose of meditation is to discipline the nervous system so that it is prepared to receive Grace.

Q) What is the use of a quiet mind?

A) Only through a quiet mind can you experience ecstasy forever.

Q) How do you know that you are in the supreme state? Can you describe it?

A) The supreme state is Self-evident. There is no question about the experience if you are having it. But the experience is indescribable. Therefore, language is useless. I can tell you that it is right there in front of you. Yes, you are swimming in it. What is the supreme state? It is just recognizing that what is simply is.

Q) How can I make my mind steady?

A) You can't. The mind is not yours. It is universal in nature. It will do what it wants.

Q) Can I avoid a protracted battle with the mind?

A) No, you can do nothing to avoid it. Mind will eat you up, swallow you whole and then spit you out. Just let it do its thing.

Q) Do you have desires or fears anymore? Aren't you afraid of death?

A) I experience what you experience only I experience it without resistance. It passes through me completely without any residue. It is just scenery. Death is also just scenery. There is no emotional charge associated with it.

Q) Are you the witness?

A) Yes, I am that beyond which there is nothing. I am the primordial source. I am eternal, unbounded and the silent witness of all.

Q) The Awakened man appears to eat, drink and so on. Is he aware of it?

A) There is complete awareness of action only there is no localized recipient of the fruits of those actions.

Q) Who is running the world?

A) I thought you were running it. You are running it, you know. It is that you just haven't realized it yet. There is an infinite aspect of you that is one with the Creator.

Q) What is power?

A) Infinite power is merging with the Self. That is Divine power. That is the power to transform anything. In contrast, temporal power is short lived. It is a flash in the pan.

Q) What is the source of consciousness?

A) Consciousness is the Self.

Q) Is silence an attribute of the real?

A) There is nothing that is not an attribute of the real. The real is the Self.

Q) How do I deal with the world's sorrows?

A) The only real way deal with the world's sorrows is to realize that you are not the sorrows. They are neutral. They are just happening. And your personal experience is an emotion charged interpretation of that experience. Seek Divine Grace in order to experience what I am talking about because it cannot be understood intellectually.

Q) Without God's power nothing can be done. Even you would not be sitting here and talking to us without him. Is there no God apart from you?

A) I am the expressed value of that which is inexpressible. Although God is God and I am me, we are inseparable.

Q) Life is so intelligent. How can it be so unconscious?

A) Life is consciousness. Unconsciousness stems from a fundamental misperception which tells us we exist apart from consciousness itself.

Q) I have studied the philosophy of many Gurus and I think that more personal development is needed before I can dream of self realization. Am I on the right track?

A) Self realization has nothing to do with the study of philosophy. Self realization is a direct experience which takes place in this moment. Intellectual preparation is unnecessary. Intellect is uninvolved with the process and can actually interfere. Divine Grace is the only cause for self realization.

Q) How does one go beyond the mind? Is such a state realizable?

A) Mind is necessary for this world. It is not useful to go beyond the mind. If you realize your Self, then your personal mind serves the Universal mind.

Q) Can you tell me which road to self realization is the shortest?

A) The sense of "to do" created the road. There was never a road. Self realization is here… now.

Q) Will meditation help me to reach your state?

A) This state is not my state. God is expressing herself through my nervous system. This occurred only through God's Grace.

Q) Realization of the eternal and the practical response to worldly events seem to be two different and separate issues. You seem to roll them into one. What makes you do this?

A) Self is inseparable from everything. Whether I am realizing the eternal or washing the dishes, it is all the same to the Self. God cannot be separated out from any experience.

Q) If I have created the world, why have made it so bad?

A) It's not bad. It is not good. It just is. But your ego is very opinionated. The God in you created the world. The ego in you created the bad.

Q) Isn't God a person?

A) Yes you are!

Q) Did you get your realization through effort or by the Grace of your Guru?

A) It is all about the Guru's Grace. You cannot become Awakened by your own efforts.

Q) Can a Guru give realization without words, without trust, without any preparation?

A) Yes, This experience is well documented in the ancient literature.

Q) Do you love the world?

A) I am the world. How could I not love myself?

Q) There are so many ignorant people in the world and so few Awakened ones. What is the cause?

A) Ignorance is a misperception and it is a puzzle to me why so few can experience this. To me, it is an obvious thing. But I remember that it was not always this way. I remember suffering. I remember that it was so unpleasant. But something happened to change it for me. Grace entered me and I was lifted out of all of this. I became free. The "I" sense changed. Grace expanded my "I" sense to incorporate the entire world. "I" became everything. Suffering vanished with the direct experience of this truth.

Q) Does the supreme state come and go?

A) The supreme state is all that there is. That is why they call it supreme. How could it come and go. Where would it go, anyway? Would it leave town? Is it going to get unsupreme? What would unsupreme even look like? The truth is that only you come and go.

Q) Do you speak from your own experience?

A) I am that. That is why it is so easy to discuss these things. There is not an intellectual process going on inside of me. I speak as the Self.

Q) How can I become universal?

A) You ARE universal. There is no becoming. How can you become what you are? Where are you right now that you do not see that you are nothing but the Supreme Self? You are the totality of existence.

Q) What is the cause of personification, of self-limitation in time and space?

A) The brain produced an experiential sense of enclosure within the physical body. Society reinforces this perception.

Q) If the Self is not the body or the mind, can it exist without them?

A) The body and the mind cannot exist without the Self because only the Self exists.

Q) Since all is pre-ordained, is our self-realization pre-ordained too?

A) Absolutely! The time and the place of your realization is fixed in stone.

Q) You sit here talking to people. What is your real motive?

A) It's simple! I want to Awaken the entire universe to Oneness.

Q) People come to you for advice. How do you know the answer?

A) I hear the answer inside me. It is there along with the question. The question and the answer seem to co-create each other.

Q) Is the universe a product of the senses?

A) Can the senses exist without the universe? It seems to me that one cannot exist without the other. They manifest simultaneously.

Q) How can I cease to be what I feel I am?

A) Whatever you feel you are is all right. There is no utility in being other than what you are. You should be authentic.

Only realize that you are not a central repository for your experiences. Experience is a non-local event happening through you. It is impersonal.

Q) Can you enter into the mind and heart of another man and share his experience?

A) I would not use the word enter because it sounds invasive. I would use the words merge or become in its place. We all need to be able to do this. We are one living being. We are a shared experience. Only, most of us are unconscious of the process.

Q) What is the link between my personal consciousness and your personal consciousness?

A) Neither is personal. That is the link.

Q) If my life is really a dream and you are a part of it, what can you do for me?

A) I can help you to live a better dream. You are suffering in your dream right now. I can help you to experience that your dream is not yours. Rather, it is a cosmic dream. It is the Creator's dream. When you come to realize this, your dream will be filled with uncontainable happiness.

Q) You say that you are in a timeless state. Does it mean that the past and the future are available to you?

A) It means that I am not on the clock. It means that, for me, there is no restriction in space/time. Think of it this way. The past and the future are both present while they are happening. I am that present.

Q) Is there a way of gaining detachment?

A) Oneness Blessing will disengage you from what is

happening to you. This will produce a state of eternal happiness in you.

Q) How can I find peace when the world suffers?

A) You need to focus on your own Self realization. Only then will you be at peace. It is not so much what is happening in the world as where you are experiencing the world from.

Q) When an ordinary man dies, what happens?

A) The body drops. The Self remains but usually there is so much guilt and previous birth momentum that we invariably choose to return. It is not necessary. God offers all of us the chance to remain with her forever in heaven but we always seem to turn her down.

Q) If you have created the world out of love, why is it so full of pain?

A) When you find love in the pain, then you will understand why I made it that way.

Q) Please tell us honestly, are you conscious or unconscious?

A) I am neither. I am in between. I am both.

Q) The seer and the seen, are they two or one?

A) They are seeking closure because they are actually one. They are eternally asking each other, "What are you doing over there?"

Q) When I ask a question and you answer, what exactly happens?

A) You momentarily transcend your body/mind.

Q) How do I find a Guru whom I can Trust?

A) You will never trust anybody until you learn to trust yourself. Trust is an issue for you, not for the Guru.

Q) Is there no end to self-discovery?

A) Self-discovery goes on forever. It has to do with the structure and function of God. God is in motion therefore, Self-realization is also in motion.

Q) Is perfection the destiny of all beings?

A) Divinity is the source of all things. All things know this. So, all things yearn to be Divine again. That is why there is always motion towards growth. There is motion toward Divinity.

Q) Why does pleasure end in pain?

A) Pleasure and pain are co-created. One could not exist without the other. They are relative to each other. We are always on a sliding scale somewhere between the two. If we are at pleasure, it has to end in something. It has to end in non-pleasure. Non-pleasure is experienced as pain.

Q) You say that whatever you see is yourself. Here is this morning's newspaper. How do you explain the suffering?

A) Suffering is not bad. That is perception. That is a notion in your mind. I am neutral. Life is neutral. It is filled with many experiences. They are all neutral. They are happening. That's it.

Q) How does one come to know the knower?

A) Stop thinking that you have to come to know anyone or anything. You ARE the knower. That is the only truth. Accept it. Grace is the only way to do this. The Divine has to step in and Awaken you to a truth that has always existed. No efforts on your part are of any use.

Q) How can I come to see myself as you see me?

A) Sit over here and I will sit over where you are. Then you will see me the way I see you.

Q) Do I need the mind to know myself?

A) You need the mind to know yourself but you do not need the mind to be yourself.

Q) When do I know that I have discovered the truth?

A) When you are the living truth, there will be no question because there will no longer be anyone to ask it.

Q) We are told that there are many levels of existence. Do you exist and function on all levels? While you are on earth, are you also in heaven?

A) There is nowhere that I do not exist. I am a function of all levels. All levels have expressed me in front of you.

Q) In the state of realization, do things change? Do they become colorful and full of meaning?

A) It can change. It can not change. Realization is unique to each nervous system. Your Realization will be in your own terms. If you are striving for the realization of the Buddha or of Ramana Maharishi, it definitely will not happen for you like that. It will be much better than that because it will be the realization that YOU always wanted. It will be perfect!

Q) How can a point become the universe?

A point is the universe! So what's your point?

Q) What makes me limited and superficial?

A) You will always be limited and superficial because the "you" is an invention of mind. Only the Self can be limitless truth.

Q) If the shape of things is mere appearance, what are they in reality?

A) The shape of everything is really the shape of God.

Q) In the whole universe, is there one single thing of value?

A) Every single thing in creation is priceless because every single thing contains every single other thing within it.

Q) What are your feelings concerning dream interpretation as a tool for Awakening?

A) I am not against dream interpretation. I am only concerned when people use dreams to color their waking experience. If dream interpretation becomes a layer of knowledge, then it will have to be discarded at some point. In the end, the goal is to have no mental baggage. The goal is to have no overlays. Life has to be lived at face value. What is simply is.

The great Lord Shiva, of Indian mythology, clearly expresses this in the second Shiva Sutras. The second Sutra states, "Knowledge is bondage". In other words, knowledge stands in direct opposition to the realization of the Self. That is why Shiva uses very few words. Lord Shiva is interested in providing the experience of the Self, not in talking about it.

This concept is very foreign to us because our western culture is based on the accumulation of knowledge. We are taught from a very early age that the more we know, the more successful we will be in our lives. This may be true for material success, but not for spiritual success. If you look, historically, at who has attained an Awakening, it has been the simple, innocent devotees. The smart guys talk the talk while simple guys walk the walk. Why is this true? It is because the Self has nothing to do with the mind. The Self is just experience. The truth is that primitive people experience an Awakening much more easily than us sophisticated intellectuals. This is because, as Christ put it, "you must be innocent like a child before you can enter the gates of heaven".

Q) What is the relationship of Awakening to non-attachment?

A) In Awakening, the experience is not so much non-attachment as it is non-relationship. You become your own center. Nothing outside of you has any use to you. This is because the outside becomes nothing other than your own self. THIS IS ALL YOUR SELF.

Q) What is the nature of Oneness?

A) Oneness has no momentum to it. It is motionless. There are no distances. There is no here to there. There is no subject relating to an object. There is no dichotomy. Because of this, there is no uneasiness. There is no sense of effort. In Oneness, the drive to get somewhere has simply disappeared.

Q) What is your core belief and how does it relate to this world?

A) I am. I believe in nothing else. I am not opposed to this world. It just is and I let it be. It plays me. I play it. I experience. I live. I die.

Q) What is the most powerful spiritual technique that I can practice? Would you be willing to teach it to us today?

A) This moment that you are in is perfect. Let me repeat this. This moment that you are in is perfect. No technique ever practiced in the history of spiritual endeavor is more powerful or more evolutionary for you than this moment already is. The Sages knew this. They new that whether they were being crowned king of the Universe or being nailed to a cross or both together; the moment that they were in was absolutely perfect. They knew that the moment, not the circumstances of the moment, was of value. The Sages knew that they had nothing to do with the content of the moment that they were in. That was God's domain. They just experienced what was happening. That's it! It's so obvious. Why do we try and try to experience everything other than what's happening? We somehow believe that this moment is flawed because it does not fit our image of what is supposed to happen. Why do we assume that we know more than God about what this moment is supposed to look like? Are we really that smart? Listen, God has done all the leg work for us. God has an agenda that is bigger than just our little piece of the action. Relax and enjoy the ride. It's better than any movie you'll ever watch.

Q) What are you experiencing right now and how is your experience different from mine. What is the cause of this difference and how do you know that it is real?

A) You may not believe it. You may call me crazy. But the fact is, I go on forever and my nature is limitless bliss. What is radiating through me touches each and every one of you and you are changed by it. A mere glance will shift you. And this takes Zero Effort on my part. There is only the infinite organizing power of Nature at work here. I walk and talk and live a life. That is true. And things do not always go in my personal favor. Or, at least, it may appear that way. The fact remains that I am that immutable force of the Divine. That is why it is so boring for me to teach "techniques" when just a single impulse in my awareness is all that is ever required.

Now, you may wonder what has happened to me that this is now my experience. Here is the best way that I can explain it. There is a Presence or Grace which permeates God's world. This Presence is God's intelligent energy for change. Humans are guided by this Presence in an unconscious manner. It is always there invisibly guiding our actions. This Presence energy flows in one direction only. It flows from God to man. So, man cannot directly access this Presence energy. This is why spiritual "techniques" are ineffective. Man can try and try from his side connect with God but it is completely up to the Divine whether the Presence or Grace descends into man.

Grace has descended into me. The Presence energy is within me and I have surrendered to it. It is not a matter of choice for me. The Grace will do as it wishes.

Now, you ask how I know that Grace has descended into me. My reply to you is that there is nothing to know; nothing to find out; nothing to do; nothing to be.

The Self is just Self-evident.

Q) Why are we so dissatisfied as a species?

A) To answer this question, we need to examine some of the preconceived notions that we hold regarding the nature of the present moment. After all, when we are dissatisfied, we are always dissatisfied in the present. To begin with, man has the unconscious belief that the present moment is in some way flawed; that the only real use for this moment is as a stepping stone to get to the next one. Because we believe that the moment is flawed, we have the idea that the next moment must be a better one; that there is hope in the next moment for overcoming the flaws contained in the present one. The fact is that for most of us, there are very, very few moments in our lives when we are not seeking the next moment. There are very few moments when we are just satisfied with what is.

What is wrong with this moment, anyway? I experience no problems, here. I am not suffering. There is no need arising in me to get away from this moment. I am content. I am satisfied. I am satisfied all of the time. Even if I am having a root canal done and I am experiencing intense pain; I am still not suffering. Another way of expressing this is that I experience no mental baggage accompanying my physical experience of the pain. I am completely the experience of the root canal simply because that's what is. The pain is just an aspect of the experience of the moment. The pain is not the moment itself. I am not lost to the moment because of the pain.

Now, I am not against the future. I am not against personal initiative. I am not against getting ahead. I am just pointing out that we have been neglecting a fundamental part of our experience; namely, the present moment. The present moment is the actual point where all of our experience takes place. Because we have neglected the moment, we have ended up with a life of searching for satisfaction through avoiding the present, when, the truth is, that satisfaction has nothing at all to do with what is presently happening to us. The truth is that satisfaction is only the experience of the present moment in which life is happening to us. The truth is that living in the present moment is synonymous with satisfaction.

Q) What is the source of all of the problems of mankind?

A) Maya, the great illusion, creates a tendency in the human mind to be in some other time rather than in the present moment. And that is the source all of the problems of mankind. The great Sages had a way of dealing with this problem. The Sages would send their devotees on a glorious wild goose chase. The devotees would be given all matter of spiritual practices and rituals to perform. The devotees would be led to believe that all of it was necessary to obtain the "Holy Grail" of spiritual experiences: Enlightenment. This would go on for years and years. After all, the devotees needed to believe that it was a long and arduous journey to reach such a lofty goal. Finally, the devotees would be ripe. They would be ready to give up in deep and utter frustration. The Sage would then say something like, "All this is that" or "That thou art" or the Sage would just a slap the devotee across the head. This would be all that was needed. The devotee would awaken to a new reality. Wrong! He would awaken to what already IS. He would awaken to the fact that THIS IS ALL THERE IS. The reason for the years and years of practice was to prove to the devotee, beyond the shadow of a doubt, that "NOTHING WORKS". The devotee would not have listened to the Sage until he had proved to himself that "NOTHING WORKS". "NOTHING WORKS" is the true path and goal of Yoga.

In the end, there is no practice. There is no philosophy. There is no path. There is no goal. This is it. Live it! Life is just experience.

Q) What is the best way to approach my life? What is of real value? Are there any secrets?

A) No matter what I say, you will misunderstand. That is the nature of Maya, the great illusion. Let's face it. Maya is just a "concrete dream". Maya looks very real, but it is completely illusory. I want to emphasize, here, that you must play this life as if it were real. I, personally practice "redneck spirituality". Although I may permanently live a deep spiritual truth, I also live my material life at full throttle. Or as Bart Simpson would put it, "Out of my way man"!

Life is much more than we could ever imagine. It is a play in which people and things come and go. It will be over. Pay attention. It will be over for you. I know it does not seem possible. It looks like you go on forever and it is just everyone else that goes away. But, looks are deceiving. You will pass. With your passing, your universe and all of the thoughts that your life was built upon will disappear. What then? Well, that's a good question. Let me make clear that what you are now, you will not be after. No body and no mind will be there. No you will be there to understand. So talking about the "afterlife" is a waste of time. Who cares? What IS of value is right here, right now.

Why do so many of you get fixated on what is not? It puzzles me. Why do you choose to live a life in a fantasyland? Your lives are built completely on faith. Faith and belief are just matter substitutes. Hope is not real. These only serve to disconnect you from your true source. This is real. Your heartbeat and your next breath are real. When you die, you are gone. It's over. My advice to you is to make matter, matter. Make this moment count.

I will tell you a great secret. Your thoughts and those of the highest beings are identical in nature. One is no better than the other. This is because all of our thoughts have the same source. The Awakened know this. They know that there are really no hierarchies. But, we have a hard time with this. Instead, we empower. We judge. We turn our noses up or we bow down. Listen! Your thoughts are as high as the highest. You must quit being in awe of the "not you". Rather, be in awe of "you". You are the Light of God. You are endless intelligence. There are no limits within you. You are the Source.

Q) Can you explain how you make choices in your own life? What is important to you? What, if anything, has changed and how can it help us in our daily lives?

A) The fact of the matter is that I don't care anymore. I guess this sounds pretty radical so I want to explain myself. Of course, I have preferences. For instance, I prefer pleasure over pain. I prefer wealth over poverty. We all desire these things. But, my relationship to these things has changed. The drive, the need to manifest a particular outcome is missing. Life is like a big joke to me now. Really, life seems like a big joke and I am having a lot of difficulty taking it seriously. Recently, I find myself challenging a lot of "sacred taboos". None of them seem real or relevant to me anymore. Mantras and faith, Gurus and "holy texts" and so on all look childish. Now, I know that these things are of great comfort to people and I do not want to interfere with their life path. Still, the fact remains, I have completely lost the need to do anything, anymore. I already feel complete.

I keep telling people that THIS IS IT. There is nothing more. But nobody listens. I understand. You don't see the big picture. You just keep putting all of your faith in other people's opinions. You never listen inside. Your truth is inside of you. Instead, you empower others to direct the course of your lives. You end up basing your life on what someone said in a book or at a seminar. You entrust fools to guide your ship. This kind of thinking has infiltrated every level of our culture. It is designed to distract you from what already is. THIS IS! This is all that you will ever need to know. No matter how great a fantasy you are currently living, know that it will inevitably lead you back to right here, right now.

Q) What is the relationship between Awakening and the manifestation of desires?

A) The common notion is that, in Awakening, you are one with all things. Therefore, the Awakened would have power over everything in creation. Any desire they have would spontaneously manifest. This sounds logical but Natural Law is not based on logic. Natural Law is based on invisible principles not available to the mind. The Awakened operate within these invisible principles. When a normal person entertains a desire, he/she experiences the desire in a personal way. It is "my" desire. There is a sense of ownership. I want this. I desire such and such.

The Awakened operate from a different frame of reference. The nature of the desire has changed. This is because the sense of "I' or "mine" has become expanded. In Enlightenment, life takes place INSIDE of you. Desire and the object of desire both happen inside of you. To the Enlightened, IT IS IMPOSSIBLE TO EXPERIENCE THE OBJECTS OF DESIRE AS PERSONAL DESIRES because there is an overriding ONENESS which pervades everything, everywhere. So the ability to put conscious attention on a "personal" desire is missing. The needs of the moment or the needs of nature become of overriding importance.

Q) Could you discuss how to manifest desires? What is the relationship between a desire and its manifestation?

A) We are manifesting our desires all day long. We desire to get up. We get up. We desire a shower. We take a shower. We desire a coffee. We make some coffee. The list goes on and on. These are "little manifestations". "Big manifestations" seem harder. Why is it harder to manifest a house than a cup of coffee? I don't know. It should be the identical process. I have a feeling that the mind is on its own. And I have a feeling that the relationship of thought and matter does not actually exist. I do not believe that there is a direct connection between the two. Rather, I have concluded that the matter world is on automatic pilot and that our control of it is really an illusion. This is why I feel manifesting "big" things is so hit or miss. Manifesting desire is Divine in nature and I suspect that prayer is the best approach to manifestation. This is because prayer transcends the independent nature of mind, thought, and matter. Prayer is just Divinity speaking to Herself.

Q) Tell us about the "Now". What is its nature? Why do you place so much importance on it?

A) Everything is "Now". It's the only truth. It's Gods secret. It's Heaven on the Earth. No matter what has befallen you, it's always encased in the Now. Within the Now are a billion details. Knowledge is glued together in the Now. Now is the healing salve of Divinity. Disease is the body living in the "then". The "then' is a construct of past. It creates delusional action. Be conscious. To be conscious is to be what is. Live what is happening. Why are you listening to this? You are missing the point. Look around you right now. That's the only thing. That's what you are here to learn. Learn it! Then, forget it! Being conscious in the Now is the only point.

Q) I feel that my wife is holding me back in my spiritual growth? What do I do to remedy this situation?

A) No one is responsible for you but you. That's the truth. You are your own choices. Events in your life are just your choices happening within your own consciousness. Others don't count. At any moment, you can choose growth or you can choose your own garbage. Your garbage is just your mind killing Divine Grace. Your garbage is just a closed mind. Blame is just your garbage imposed on other people. Blame is delusion. Listen! This is your movie. You wrote it. So, don't blame others. Avoid blamers, and, by all means, don't accept the blame of others.

Q) Why do we all spend so much time, energy, and money looking for a solution to our problems? What is your solution?

A) People want a cure. They want different. They want better. But, it will never happen. Life on Earth is just as you see it now. So, I preach acceptance. I say, this is it. Accept it! Surrender to it because there is absolutely, positively no alternative.

Now, this may seem like a big downer to some. But, think

about it. Life becomes very simple. Life becomes very full and complete. Nothing is missing. It is all here for you right now. There is no more wasted time seeking what might be. BE HERE NOW. That's the answer. Of course, this implies that there ever was a question in the first place.

Q) Say I want to be like Gandhi or Martin Luther King. Is it healthy to strive to be like other people?

A) You have to love yourself. You have to love who you are. Be who you are. Evolution can only be in terms of who you were born to be. Don't be someone else. No matter how cool someone else is, they are not you. You were born to live your own life. Living another's life is a complete waste. You cannot grow. You will be stuck and it won't be fun. Even if you achieve the world, it will be someone else's world and you will feel unfulfilled.

When you are just you, you are complete. There is this synchronicity that happens. Some nerve pathways open up and your relationship with everything just clicks. It flows. It is full and integrated. It is not on the level of thought. There is no thinking involved. It is outside your personal choice. You are doing what you were born to do so whatever you do or don't do, it is done to perfection. That is the true meaning of success. That is the true meaning of fulfillment. Harmony dominates. Life remains as it is, only, you are able to roll with it better. You are less reactionary. You are quiet more. You move on subtle cues. A deep Presence now emanates from you. It permeates your world. You can feel it radiating off of you. You have become a Presence transmitter. Wherever you go, the Presence is your companion. Everyone is influenced. Everyone is transformed. You do nothing. Just be and that is enough.

Q) How can I manifest my desires? How does it work?

Can you teach us a technique?

A) You can intend what you want. It's easy. The trick is to understand the mechanism of manifestation. Manifestation is intent plus leverage. Desire it. Picture it in your mind. That is intent. Leverage makes energy come alive. The leverage is the sound "Ah". "Ah" is motion, magnetic motion between the pictured desire and the physical expression of the desire. "Ah' lights a fire under the picture. The picture shakes. It vibrates and becomes unstable. The picture seeks homeostasis by becoming physical. It slows down. It becomes heavy and falls. The picture falls into the physical. It finally lands near you but you must look to find it. To you, the manifestation of your desire is a coincidence. But it is just the technology of intent and leverage and it is absolutely perfect.

Q) I still have trouble with concept of choice and free will. Could you talk more about it?

A) You are fixed. You are set in your ways and you have no choice. So, any advice that I may impart will be just an "added vice" to you and you will not listen. You will do what you want. Your programming leaves no room for you to break out. It is beyond either of our capacity to circumvent this reality. I will act. You will act. It is as though we are both working from a script. I will push your buttons. You will push mine. And the funny thing is that we will both believe that we have control over our interaction. This is delusion. We have done this for-ever and we will continue to do this forever. It is unchange-able. It is Destiny. It is Cosmic Law.

Q) Why is it so hard to change our destiny?

A) First of all, our destiny is based on how we perceive our world. And, if you think about it, all of our choices are just a reaction to our perceptions. Our perceptions are biologically based, i.e., perception of an object is a neurobiologic event.

What I mean by this is that we perceive the object from within our central nervous systems. And, our central nervous systems, in turn, are matter-based. And the bottom line is that matter changes very, very slowly. Destiny, which is matter-based, changes very, very slowly. The bioelectrical signals must be changed. The neurology must rewire itself. The matter within us must reorganize itself in order to reflect a completely new paradigm. It would follow that Awakening, the ultimate destiny change, is just a reflection of re-arranged body matter. I personally believe that no two Awakenings will be the same because no two chemistries are the same. No two DNA sequences are the same. In the end, both nature and nurture will contribute to shape a unique Awakened destiny for each of us.

Q) How does the sense of "I" relate to the present moment? Who is the "I" anyway? Is the "I" real?

A) I like to define life as a collection of "present" moment experiences occurring one right after the other. They have no real intrinsic value and they are happening for just no good reason at all. These "present" moment experiences are raw input, registered by the senses and translated into chemical signatures within the body. Now, you asked if there is an "I" that experiences these "present" moment experiences. The truth is that thoughts, mind, body and personality, those things that make up the "I", all operate independently of one another. So the idea of a cohesive "I" at our center is an illusion. Even our mind and our thoughts are not generated from within us. Rather, they are part of the, ancient, universal sphere of the mind. There is just one mind transmitting an infinite number of thoughts through six billion "thought receivers". So trying to get anywhere spiritually is a problem. For instance, how do I develop my mind and improve my thinking if my mind and thoughts are not my own? How do I evolve my body if my body runs without being under my direct control? Which one of my personalities gets enlightened, anyway? And just how do I go about enlightening all of them? The fact of the matter is that there can be no enlightenment for me because there was never a "me" to enlighten in the first place. I just exist and none of what is happening to me is within my control. I am and there is nothing but what is right now. I am. You are. This is and that's it. It is so, so simple.

Q) How is the Divine Presence related to the "Now"?

A) So much is happening in the "Now" and we are aware of so very little of it. The pace of the "Now' is driven by the Divine Presence. If I feel the Presence within me, I know that I am connected to the pace of the "Now'. God lets me know the pace by the waves of bliss within the Presence, which is within me. Although the Presence is within me, I am also deeply lost in it. There is little distinction between us anymore. We are within each other. We carry each other. We speak for each other. We are identical twins; yet we are different. It is not a concept available to the human mind. Although our relationship is absolutely complete, it is still growing. No end to it is in sight. It is a love affair. We would do anything for each other. I love my Divine friend beyond all measure. We are One but two. We are One and we are two because it takes two to complete the One. It takes two to link the One. Who is speaking these words? I am and the Presence is as well! We are both speaking because we are the One.

Q) Can you tell us a formula for making right choices?

A) It's hard to make choices. We all stress a lot over them. Why is this? Why is it so hard to make choices? It is because each choice contains a degree of truth. This is because every choice has the same source: Pure Consciousness. The degree of correctness of a choice is based on its level of consciousness, i.e., the level of purity of that choice. The most pure choice is the one which is closest to Natural Law. What is Natural Law? Natural Law is simply what is supposed to happen at any given moment. Choices are polarities. They are connected. They cannot exist independent of each other. Each choice has an energy which is intrinsic to it. This energy is created by its relationship to the opposing choice. There is truth in every choice. Even the greatest falsehood has truth. Remember, the greatest truth can exist only with the support of the greatest falsehood. So how do we deal with choices?

First, any choice is better than no choice.

Second, any choice is correct, so don't worry so much. You can't really make a mistake. There are no mistakes. There are just opportunities to grow.

Third, think about both options. Think of one choice and then think of the other, separately. Note: It would be good to deep meditate before doing this. Now, close your eyes and quietly look inside. Look at both choices with your minds eye. One of the choices will look and feel lighter. Go with that choice. It is the higher choice. It is closest to Natural Law. It will be of maximum benefit to you and to your world.

Fourth, you should leave the rest to God. Let God handle the details. Do not entertain doubt or remorse. It was the right choice.

Fifth, you must do your part to manifest your choice. Remember. God helps those that help themselves.

Q) You sometimes refer to Maya, the illusion, as the "Web". Can you explain the "Web" to us?

A) We are all encased in a "Web" which connects everything to everything else. If one person moves, all the others will feel it by means of the "Web". We may not be conscious of it, but we will all be influenced nonetheless. The "Web" is made up of innumerable threads. There is a thread for each and every action. By observing an individual's tendency toward a certain style of action, a Yogi can follow the threads related to these actions over time, to determine any potential outcome for the individual at any point in the future. In other words, a Yogi can see a person's future by following the trends of the threads. The Yogi can then positively influence the outcome for an individual by putting his attention on changing the tendency of certain threads. Everything in spirituality operates through the manipulation of the threads of the "Web". Religious rituals can move it. Great souls can move it. The whole of higher states development is associated with "Web" manipulation. The "Web" is often referred to as Maya. It is driven by desire and made physical through attention. It creates the localized expression of the Universal Mind. When we become one with the "Web", we are never alone again. Even the edge of the universe becomes as close as our own physical body. The potential to transform the Earth into Heaven is possible if we can just understand the relationship of the thread to the "Web". The threads are polarized strands. Each individual thread is created out of extremes. We travel the length of the threads from one extreme to another through action. But the goal is always the same; pleasure, happiness, the absence of pain.

The Third Eye contains within it, a blueprint for the entire "Web". The Third Eye is like a switching station between the Localized Self and the Universal Self. A Yogi can examine any aspect of the "Web" through his/her Third Eye and by attention and intention, can shift the polarities of certain threads to modify reality. Reality, in this context, can be thought of as a series of dreams constructed out of polarized threads of Consciousness. Awakening is just being conscious of the Oneness of the polarities. Finally, God is the "Web" and Grace is the tendency of God to reveal Her totality to any of Her parts.

Q) I find some of the things you talk about very hard to grasp. Sometimes I find myself resisting it. Why is this?

A) When I teach, it is to your Soul. But this is not your experience and you are skeptical. What I am describing does not gel with your experience. It sounds, vague, fanciful, crazy, dreamy, and not very practical. It sounds that way because your mind has never given you a moments rest. It is like trying to describe a dream to someone who has never dreamt before.

Q) How does Karma affect our choices?

A) On any given day, we act from a program which exists within our Soul. Actually, this program is located just above our Soul, in the area of our intellect. We are like billiard balls. Our Soul-based program causes us to continually interact with every atom in the entire universe. Our programmed actions, which occur in perfect harmony and in perfect sequence, eventually bounce back to their origin and affect their originator. This is the law of Karma. Our Karma is unavoidable because we are, in a sense, condemned to live out our program. Choice, then, is not really a choice. Choice is just part of the original program. Now, in extreme cases, our program can be overridden. Buddha, through intense moment awareness, overrode his program. He was born to be a prince but, through pure unbroken attention, he made himself into a Buddha; an Awakened One.

Think this to yourself. "I am the goal. I override my present circumstance; my program. I tap into the energy of the Creator and through attention only, I change my role. I utilize the energy of the Infinite moment. This moment transcends time. It is the time of Creator before his Creation. I am forever this holy moment. I am a holy person in this holy moment".

Q) What is the relationship between Awakening and

Divine Grace?

A) You awaken yourself but Grace allows it to take place. Without Grace, there is no way to get out of this bondage. Grace is light. Grace is not of this world. No set of actions can create Grace. Grace is independent of action. How do we receive Grace then? There is no technique and nothing you can do to make it happen. Again, Grace is independent of this World. (I personally endorse the Oneness Deeksha or Oneness Blessing as a direct means of receiving Grace. Refer to Appendix I for details)

Q) We are told that the ego is opposed to our spiritual development. What do you think about this?

A) I am not a fan of ego destruction. Ego is necessary to live this life. You need to feed your family. You need ego based desire to live and learn. You can live "Heaven on Earth" and still entertain desires. Matter is not opposed to liberation. There is liberation in matter. After all, matter and spirit have the same source.

Q) Do you have any predictions about the fate of the world?

A) There is a lot driving the moment. Better than 90% of it is unseen. There is an ocean of underlying energies driving everything. These are not your thoughts. They are the product of a collective consciousness interacting with itself to fulfill the ultimate purpose. Free will does not operate here. Conditioning from many, many lifetimes will force you to act as though you were a robot. Occasionally, great souls will come and wake you up. But it is short-lived. Entropy will tend to make the experience unclear and will eventually lead to doubt. You are doomed to fall away from the light again and again. But some day the light will not fade anymore. Doubt will be replaced by complete surrender to the moment. Pray for that day. It is beyond any of us to interfere right now. We will soon witness a renaissance. Life will be quite different afterwards. Suffering, the hallmark of the earth plane, will lessen significantly. It will usher in an era where mind controls matter.

Q) Can you explain to me who I really am?

A) You are wholeness. You are the moment. You would do well not to judge it. It is just you within you by you and for you. You are one with the Creator. Know it as only you. You are self- contained. Even if you are killed, know that you killed you and fundamentally you have not changed. You are still you. Who are you? The question really is, who are you not? Now, there is a paradoxical you. It is local and non-local simultaneously. Learn to live both without conflict. Just know that there is a non-local you that can affect the local you. You do not lose your completeness. Only, you can now operate more freely within your completeness. In other words, you can glorify your completeness.

Q) Can you talk to us about Psychic or Spiritual powers? Can they develop all at once?

A) There is a point in one's evolution when all of the Spiritual or Psychic "Supranormal" powers can develop at once, spontaneously. This type of development is just a byproduct of the Oneness. It is a generalized power. It is very different from the more common Psychic abilities that express themselves in some individuals. Usually, these abilities, such as clairvoyance, clairaudience or telekinesis, are limited. Maybe one or two are expressed and the individual must use ATTENTION and INTENTION to utilize them. But I am speaking of a power that is not limited in its expression. It is Omnipresent, Omniscient, and Omnipotent. NO awareness is necessary for its expression. This power acts on your behalf without any conscious effort. It is the Power of Powers.

Q) Why is it so difficult to remain in the moment?

A) We all believe that there is something more. We are so goal oriented. The present circumstances are just something to be overcome so that the better future can arrive. But when the future finally gets here, it looks suspiciously like the present. It will never, ever be any different. This is this. It will always be exactly like this. Always! Nothing will ever fit right. Things will be just a little off. There will always be some tension or charge. A little discomfort will always be felt.

But beauty is there also. All of it is so beautiful. If you could only stop and become your experience, you would see how beautiful this moment is. Look at the form of the words on the page. Experience the colors, the sounds, the tastes, and the smells. Each is artistic perfection. They are beyond perfection. They are Divine. Stop! Stop! Stop! Nothing you are doing right now is as important as stopping, feeling, being. The world will all be there when you get back because it is never ending. When you stop, even for a minute, Divinity infuses into you and you will carry some of it back into your life.

Q) Why are some people luckier than others? Why do some people have an easier time manifesting what they want?

A) Manifestation is just a formula. This formula involves light. This light produces attraction. It doesn't matter what you think. It doesn't matter what you do. The light will do it. The light will organize a sequence of events to put you in the right place at the right time. This light is the light of "Dumb Luck". No matter what you do, if you have, "Dumb Luck", you will make money and get pleasures. It is a kind of Grace. It is a quality of Divinity. The "Dumb Luck" light is unique. It is high, silent, and very smart. After all, it has to be so smart that you can afford to be dumb.

Q) Why is there conflict? Why is there resistance to our desires?

A) It is clear that our lives hinge on elements that are beyond our control. Something beyond us is moving us. We are all being moved by a single process and nothing can stop this group process from unfolding. We are not in control of even our next thought. But negotiations are now taking place. Some Divine Beings, some yogis, shamans, etc. are negotiating with God on behalf of the human race. It is beyond our capacity to understand what is happening but we can be appreciative and pray for Grace.

Q) What is the nature of healing? How does it work?

A) Healing is a matter of applying a Divine Connection. Two things are necessary. First, the Divine must initiate this connection and second, it must completely control it. The healer must become a remote observer. There cannot be any conscious manipulation of the healing relationship. Healing is a blessing occurring through you. You are not directly involved. Healing is a matter of Love. The healer must Love and surrender to both the Divine as well as to the one receiving the healing Grace. The healing does not involve you, the healer. The individual "you", is not an active participant. Healing is a matter of being, not doing. Doing created the problem. The being is the healing. Many vehicles can be employed to transmit healing Grace. For instance, you can use touch, sight, or intent. You can use literally any type of mental impulse to carry healing Grace. Anything you can imagine can carry it. The power of Grace is only limited by our imagination. Imagine this!

Q) No matter how hard I concentrate, I can't seem to get

anywhere in my spiritual practice. Why is this?

A) Effort is opposed to evolution because effort bends the Laws of Nature. Because of this, effort creates more Karma. So effort has no place in spiritual practice. Control is unnatural. Nature does not control. In Nature, everything flows seamlessly and so should we. Heaven is effortless in nature. To get from Earth to Heaven, we can "do" nothing. We don't "do" heaven, rather, we "be" heaven. Heaven is achieved be neither doing nor not doing. Both require effort. The Buddha was right. Take the "Middle Path". Only, the "middle" has been misunderstood. It is neither effort, nor non-effort, nor in between these two. The "Middle Path" is indescribable and accessible only through Grace.

Q) What is the nature of desire?

A) When we desire something, there are a billion links to our desire which we are not aware of. They will have little to do with our actual conscious desire. They are Universal Movements or old karmas which create an uncontrollable attraction to the object of desire. They lay deep in the unconscious. They are non-verbal archetypes. They are located in the Chit, a Sanskrit term for the source of life impressions. Freud referred to this area of the mind as the Id. It is a very subtle, intuitive, and emotionally charged area of the unconscious. The truth of this area of the unconscious is that nothing is ever what it seems. That is, what we believe our motives are for any action has little to do with our actual motives. This is because the actual source is just too painful and guilt ridden to deal with consciously. Even if it was exposed for a moment, the individual may respond in an intensely defensive and potentially aggressive manner.

Q) How would you describe your experience of the "Now"?

A) I am a captive of the moment. I am a prisoner of the present. There is no escape. I am always awake. No one can comprehend the power; the awesome majesty; the brilliant expanded presence of this moment. I am always here. I am always now. It has become a way of life; sort of like breathing. But the world is asleep. Everyone is dreaming. I look at them, but nobody is home. Yes, they appear awake, but it is just conditioning. Their Souls remain asleep. For most, living what is not, is somehow more engaging, more dramatic, more intellectually stimulating, than just being with what is.

Q) What do you feel your role is in this world?

A) I want to tell you that you are dreaming and that I have one purpose; I am here to wake you up. I am awake in your dream. I am a reflection of your Soul. I am the Light of God. I am the light of your world. I am unmoving. No motion exists within me. I am flawless. I am just a mirror. I reflect you. You don't react to me. You react to yourself. You are only your experience. You are only absolute, infinite, and eternal bliss. Experience the dream fully, but know that you are not the dream. You are just the dreamer; the witness. Come to me. Enjoy my bliss. There is just one great Soul. There is just One Love. Find it in silence. That is the key. God and silence are one. It is not your thoughts that are important. Experience is life. Experience is not your thoughts. Rather, Life is what happens to you in between your thoughts. Thoughts are just an interpretation of the gaps between your thoughts. The gaps are important. Silence is important.

Q) Is there a time when we will not need to perform a spiritual practice?

A) Once the awareness becomes inextricably concentrated in the Self, the need for "techniques" or "advice" ceases. The Self simply overtakes the devotee. The Self becomes the teacher. The techniques manifest internally now. It is the highest teaching. There is no longer a gap between teacher and student. It is all knowledge spontaneously experienced in the moment. All forms of ancient wisdom come alive. Knowingness reveals the truth of all spiritual disciplines.

Q) Is surrender to the teacher or Guru necessary for my evolution?

A) Giving in and growing are the same act. Being humble is important because we must be nothing to be everything. Humble is only humbling to the delusional self. The Higher Self is already so humble that nobody can even locate it. We all believe that we will lose personal control of our lives if we surrender. This is a false notion. We actually gain control. Only the Higher Self is really in control, anyway. If we can't surrender, then our whole life controls us and we will never be happy.

Surrender is not a thought. Surrender is a direct experience. The experiencer vanishes. That is surrender. The greatest surrender is to live in the Now. We surrender our past and future to accomplish the Now. We are then just the experience.

Q) How should we treat the world?

A) Always favor the world. Favor living. Don't be a space cadet. Being spaced out is really being in hell. Heaven is being grounded. Take your time. Smell the coffee and the roses. Don't try to figure it all out. You can't. You need Grace to do that. You need God's intervention. In the meantime, live what you know. You should live comfort. You should desire comfort. You should crave what appeals to you. These desires are healthy. Until you are fulfilled, you can't move on. These desires are longstanding from ages past. Pamper your body. Feed it good things. Food is thought in matter form. So eat fresh thoughts. You came from light, air, water, and earth. Spend time with these things. They made you.

Q) Are there limits to the human mind?

A) The Self is limited by what the mind can imagine. We deliberately limit our potential. We are limitless. We can accomplish everything. We can be anywhere. We can do anything. That is a fact. We are the Co-creators of this universe. We hold the keys to unlock any door. The choice is ours. Bondage is just a choice. Liberation is also just a choice.

Q) Why is faith necessary?

A) If you do not have faith, then nothing good can ever happen for you. I am like a huge ocean of energy ready to be tapped into. But you need to hook up the pipeline to it. It is there. All your dreams can be fulfilled. You have to choose it. You have to choose it wholeheartedly. You must be innocent like a child. A child carries no expectations. A child doesn't think. A child feels with a pure heart. You have to let it in. It is there. Grace is there. Healing will be there. Miracles can happen. You just need the faith of a mustard seed. That is all.

Q) Can there be an Awakened society?

A) Society is an agreed upon reality. It is a sociobiological feedback loop. It is our own self-fulfilling prophecy. It is our bondage. But everyone lives a different version of this reality. This reality is reinforced, father to son, mother to daughter, generation after generation. This reinforced knowledge structures our DNA. There is no way out because the dream keeps reinforcing itself. The Awakened are awake within the societal dream. They challenge it. They kill the patterning effect of our agreed upon delusion. Their love kills delusion. Their love is unfragmented being. Their love is the ultimate. Inhale their love; soft as a rose petal. Their love is issuing forth and enveloping you in Grace. Live your life within the Awakened. "Aham Brahmasi".

Q) Gurus tell us that it is necessary to control our urges. Is control really necessary for our evolution?

A) Many people are in a mad, desperate, race to gain Awakening. I see friends of mine every day who are afraid to indulge their desires. They spend the balance of their lives unfulfilled. The thoughts are there. The desires are there. But they are not being met. That is why most spiritual people seem mentally and socially unnatural. Let me be very clear about this, only Divine Grace can create desirelessness. Only then can one truly become desireless, desire-free.

Q) How fixed is our destiny? Can it be changed?

A) We all have a destiny which pre-exists the beginning of time. From start to finish, our lives are already defined for us to the finest detail. All of our experiences of pleasure, pain, joy and sorrow are already written in stone. Every thought is orchestrated. Our lives unfold with such precision. We are like robots, in that we respond so predictably to our own programming. That is why change, a fundamental life-altering change, is impossible without Divine intervention.

Q) I've made a lot of mistakes in my life. If I change my thinking, can I change my life? Is there another way to change?

A) It is not your fault. You are not what is happening to you. Your thoughts are not your own and your actions are not within your control. Life is happening within itself. This is our human drama. It is our own special blend. You are the experience only! You are here to watch and play and nothing you can do will make it better for you. You cannot think your way out of this one because you are not really thinking your thoughts. Grace must happen to you. God must intervene and lift you out. It is up to God as to when this will happen. God does not care what you have done up to now. God's love for you is beyond limits. So, again, don't feel badly. It is not your fault.

Q) How do you know that you know?

A) I don't know and I don't care. Knowing gets in the way of knowing. It is a blessing to forget what we know. The more we know, the more karma we carry. Don't try to interpret. Life is and that is enough. Life already knows everything about itself. We can supply nothing. And life is waiting to supply us with everything. Living is the solution to life. There is nothing to know; nothing to find out; nothing to do; nothing to be or not be. That is already done for us. God has figured it out perfectly. But we doubt God and doubt is the non-God. Doubt is the Devil. Doubt is the ego trying to outsmart God. Life is already perfect! Children know this intuitively. This is why Christ advises us to be innocent like a child if we wish to enter the gates of Heaven.

Q) What is important to you personally?

A) What happens to me is unimportant. Whether I gain or lose does not touch me. I am That. All this is nothing but That. My way is just a way. It is a point of view based on a notion of selfhood; lifetimes in the making. We all have our way and I bow to your way.

Q) What is the nature of relationships? How do they relate to our spiritual development?

A) All relationships are just a re-enactment of the relationship with our parents. And the parental relationship is always bittersweet. Forgiveness is the healing ointment. Forgive yourself. It's not your fault. Forgive your parents. It wasn't their fault either. Everyone here is involved in karma delivery. It comes with the territory. Ask God to help you to love and to ask for love. Our success in the world is dependent on healing this primordial wound. Spiritual growth cannot proceed unless we address our relationship with the original "other"

Q) How should spiritual people live in this material world?

A) Spiritual people need to make matter, matter. Think and act. Desire and act. Imagine beautiful things, crave a good life. Luxury is good. Poverty is not so good in this modern world because evolution has become very expensive. Comfort means no distractions and the goal requires no distractions. So it is not a sin to desire a comfortable ride. Rather, it is a blessing.

Q) Could you discuss the nature of relationships a little more? What is the cosmic significance? Is it a spiritual path?

A) The past is the glue which binds relationships together. The familiar creates a loving attraction. A relationship is an easy dance which gives a brief respite from life's uncertainties. The uneasiness of relationships stems from the struggle, in both partners, between the selfless and the selfish. Relationship is primordial. Each partner carries an ancient gap. Each is incomplete without the other. Each gap can only be filled by the other. Surrender is the fundamental goal of relationship. We sublimate our needs for our beloved. Relationship is a spiritual path. In relationship, we culture an awareness of unity by seeing the other as we see our own self. It is higher states path. It is a path of devotion. Our beloved becomes our guru. Our beloved becomes the goal of our devotion. In the end, we vanish and only our beloved remains.

Q) "Where there is a will there is a way", is a well known saying. How does willing something relate to manifestation?

A) What a wonderful truth. A will is an intention. I intend

an outcome. I envision a reality. I dream it. My dream is a blueprint. I keep dreaming the same dream. Over and over, I see it with my inner vision. My dream is unbroken. My dream becomes my reality. No difference exists anymore. I am my dream. I am no longer dreaming. I am awake in my dream. I am awake and there is no longer a dreamer. And there is no longer a dream.

Q) How do I solve problems in my life?

A) There is no a solution to the problems of life. Life is just experience and you are just an observer. You are never really connected to your actions. Actions are simply not your fault, rather, they are Self-engendered interactions. So you cannot solve your life because there is nothing to solve and no one to solve it.

Q) If I am not always present, where am I when I am not present?

A) Why are we absent to the present? Was the present really present, while we were absent? Would we have to be absent to see if the present was present while we were absent? And if we were not present in the present, where were we? Wouldn't we be present in the absent? If so, then, would we still be absent? And who would be absent anyway? To me, there is no real absence in the absent because the reason we were absent to the present is that we were present to the absent.

Q) What is blame? Is it a necessary part of living?

A) We all blame each other for our lot in life. In a way, it is true. The other is doing it to us. But the truth is that ourselves and the other complete a cycle of interaction. We are both essential. What is important is not ourselves or the other, but the cycle of experience between us both. The Self interacts with Itself, by Itself and for Itself.

Q) Who was I in a past lifetime?

A) Look at your life, your beliefs, your friends, your face, and your attitudes. They are your past in present form. They are you recycled. Want to change? Delete your past and future. Things may continue to happen to you, but the sense of you will be transformed.

Q) Does what we do for a living in this world relate to our evolution?

A) We all believe that we are what we do in this world. This is the source of the great mistake. The truth is that we are only what does not change at all in our lives. The rest is just experience playing itself out on the screen of our consciousness. We actually act without acting. The Awakened live this truth. They are conscious of the actors and the script. They know and admire the director. The Awakened live their lives sitting in a comfortable seat, observing the screen of their consciousness, with popcorn and a cold drink in hand. Therefore, I do not love what you do. I love who you are. I love your essence. You essence is not touched at all by what happens to you in your life. That will never be under your control. Who you are IS you. You are the observer in each moment. You are what is left over after the rest of your life crumbles around you. What is left is God. What is left is God as the observer. That is why I love and bow to you again and again. I bow to the God in you.

Q) What is the nature of the present moment?

A) Within the moment, there is no possibility for corruption. The moment is out of time. The moment is out of mind. The moment is untainted by thoughts, opinions, notions or concepts. It is unlimited and unfathomable. The moment is God's entry point. In the moment, subject and object merge. The dynamic tension between the two disappears, and with it, the source of all ignorance.

Q) What is your responsibility to the planet?

A) My responsibility to the planet is to just be; nothing more. Being is the highest seva. I love you all with all of my heart. You are the children of God. There is so much more than you can know. You only know suffering; only your own suffering. I know happiness; only happiness. Happiness is Divinity in action. Happiness is practical Divinity.

Q) They call life a waking dream? What do you suggest I do until I wake up?

A) You are dreaming and I advise you to live a comfortable dream. Don't be too extreme in any direction. Be easy with yourself. Be easy with the goal. Dream up your best dream. Desire your favorite desire and let go. When you finally wake up, it will be from your own dream, in your own way. Though your dream may continue, you will be forever awake within it.

Q) What do you think of spirituality as it is practiced today?

A) YOU ARE ALREADY GOD! That's the only point. You alone have created this incredibly difficult, painful, and time consuming path to what is already you. Listen, feel, taste, touch, smell and see. It's all you are. You are the only one. You have broken yourself into a billion pieces which are all opposed to each other. Hey! Wake up! It's all one piece. The illusion is the many. You are the one. You are the source of the many.

Q) What is the answer?

A) Be conscious. Be attentive. Be alert. Right now! Be right now! None of the rest matters. Now matters. What "is" is only in the present. What "was" is not now. What "is" cannot occur twice. It is impossible. Trying to create a "will be" out of an "is", is crazy. "Is", is my Guru. "Is", is my God. That IS it!

Q) What is the power of Maya?

A) The illusory power of Maya goes very deep. Because of Maya, truth looks like darkness and darkness looks like truth. This is why I have always maintained that given a choice, the disciple will always choose the televised picture of Niagra Falls, even while sitting right next to the actual falls. Of course, Niagra Falls here represents an Awakened One while the televised picture represents a second hand description of an awakened experience.

Q) How should I experience the moment? How are my actions related to it?

A) Relax and enjoy. Observe what is happening to you this moment. Look around. You are connected to everything, everywhere. Nothing can unfold properly without its connection to you. The Universe can only express itself perfectly at this moment by your being exactly where you are, doing exactly what you are doing. Look around again. You are in a Divine moment. You are fulfilling a vital role. Appreciate it. It may seem trivial or uncomfortable but you are, in fact, a Divine Co-creator. Enjoy this moment. You have labored from the beginning of time just to be where you are at this very moment. You are now in the Holy Temple of the Moment and your undivided attention is your offering. Namaste.

Q) There is a lot of ignorance in the world? What can be done about it?

A) Ignorance is bliss. It is true. Sometimes clueless is a good thing. After all, we can't complicate things that we are not even aware of. For this reason, I love salt of the earth folks. They have no pretenses. There is no phoniness. There is no "better than you are" attitude. Earthy folks have none of these fancy food restrictions. They are easygoing family-types. They take things in stride. Earthy folks love to have fun. They have a great time living life as it is. Just bring me, chips, a soda, fries, football, pizza, and a party hat!

Now, I'm not knocking spirit. Spirit is a big part of it. Spirit is fine. Spirit is sacred, source, sight, safe, silly and sattvic. Spirit is long-lasting. It lasts forever. Ignorance is based on the notion of permanence. Ignorance is a good short-term fix. Ignorance is like a vacation from growth. Some time, we will have to repay the debt for our ignorance, but just make payments.

Q) How do you think I should live my life?

A) I suggest a natural life. Take your time. Maybe you should take a lifetime off. Get mellow. See beauty. It's all relative, anyway. Just know that God loves you and thinks of you often. And she definitely doesn't care if you were naughty or nice. So choose an enjoyable life.

Q) How should I act around an Awakened One?

A) If you are around an Awakened One, one of two things will happen. Either you will eventually become the mind of the Awakened One, through force of habit, or you will try to fight his/her mind (the Creator's mind) and leave. There is no middle ground.

Q) What is the relationship of the present moment to mental health?

A) Now is the ultimate test of sanity. Now is the pivotal experience of consciousness. All else in your life may be in ruins, but if you are supremely concentrated in the Now, you are free. You are more comprehensive than any experience you can have. In the Now, all experience occurs within you, not outside of you. Therefore, you are always larger than anything that is happening to you.

Q) I am afraid of the Gurus' power to control their disciples. How do I deal with it?

A) No one can control anyone else. No Guru can control us or influence us unless we choose to be controlled. The hardest thing to make people understand is that we are all COMPLETELY FREE. But we all unconsciously choose bondage.

Q) Why are there so many problems?

A) People freeze a version of life which suits them and expend all of their energy trying to make Nature fit it. That is the source of all of our problems. Nature is beautiful. She is boundless and infinitely flexible. She is the great teacher. She stops for no thing because all things are essentially her. Life is not a frozen lake. Rather, life is an ever-changing river.

Q) Gurus are always promising that their disciples will gain Awakening and then be able to manifest whatever they want in the world? Is this really true?

A) There is a notion among disciples that they will gain Awakening and have all these powers and run around and manifest anything they please. And if they manifest these things, then they must be good for the whole world. It doesn't work like that. When you get these powers, it is with the understanding that NO ONE can know that you are using them. You must be completely invisible. You can never take credit for anything you do.

Q) How important is it to keep a promise?

A) We all make promises but few of us keep them. Why? It is because we are asleep when we make them. We don't pay attention. We are not awake. We do not see that the others are ourselves in disguise. There is no difference. So always promise the other as you would want to be promised. Promise is another name for manifestation. It puts the Universe on notice that a need must be fulfilled. A promise is deeply spiritual. A promise kept is an act of deep love and devotion.

Q) How does a Guru attract the right disciples?

A) When a Guru wishes to attract particular disciples, he first constructs an energy field around them. The Guru, then, establishes a link between himself and each of the chosen ones. The Guru's attention literally changes the style of thoughts that the disciples experience. By doing this, the disciples constantly entertain thoughts of the Guru. Also, this enables the Guru to protect the disciples from their own ignorance. The devotees feel empowered to overcome any obstacle to get to the Guru. The Guru sets a sequence of events in motion which directs the laws of Nature to deliver the disciples to the Guru. The disciples, literally, live the Guru's dream. Gurus will also send higher beings, made of light, to bless and direct the devotees. This is usually experienced, by the devotees, as a high pitched whining sound at the right ear.

When we have attention on the Guru, We are really attending to our own Soul. The Guru is just an easy symbol for our Soul. After all, a human form is most familiar to us. This is why it is said that we Awaken ourselves. The Guru does nothing but remind us of who we already are. We are That. The Guru is also That. Only, the Guru knows he is That and we don't. If distraction is the Devil, then unbroken attention is sainthood. Unbroken attention is Grace in action. The Guru creates such a loving attraction that the disciple can't keep his mind off the Guru. Through this process of Divine obsession, the disciple's attention eventually becomes unbroken.

Q) What's an Avatar? Is an Avatar more powerful than a

Guru? What's the difference?

A) An Avatar is a God-man. Unlike the Guru, who started out ignorant, the Avatar was never ignorant. His/Her power to transform is immeasurable. The Avatar has never been of this world. There was never a human mind; a limited selfish identity. So there was never corruption or the experience of limitation. In India, it is said that the power of a thousand Gurus can fit on the fingernail of an Avatar. I suspect that this is a gross understatement.

Q) How do we stay in harmony with Nature?

A) The more pure we are, the more we are in tune with natural law. Purity means harmony. Nature, then, steps up to the plate to support us. Harmony is complete surrender to the moment. Harmony means never judging what is happening to us in that moment. What is happening to us is perfect. Nature could not evolve without it. Nature has planned this moment from the time of the birth of our Soul.

Q) How can I enhance the speed of my evolution toward Awakening?

A) The whole idea of evolution is fatally flawed. Evolution is a mental concept which implies the necessity of change in order to become complete. This notion is crippling. Why? You are already complete. You are completely full right now. Right this instant, you are fullness and you can do nothing more to complete yourself. I will tell you a secret. You are already Awakened, but you are dreaming. You are presently sitting with the Creator, watching a video of your last lifetime before you became Awakened. But the video is very engaging, and you have become absorbed into the drama. But it is not real. You are already finished the journey. It's just a movie.

So, find the thread. The movie is held together by an invisible thread. There is a non-changing thread that ties everything together. Perfect silence is the nature of this thread. This silence constitutes the gap between any two things. Just be attentive to the gap rather than to the things. Then you will wake up and you will see that you were dreaming. You will see that the witness, the true you, has always been complete and that you were always Awakened.

Q) What is our true nature?

A) We are not of this world. We are actually completely uninvolved. So, all that we touch, all that we feel, all that we think and all that we do has absolutely nothing to do with us. We are wordless awareness.....just pure consciousness.

Yes, we have created a convincing movie. But, in reality, we are the director, the projector, and the movie screen. We have always had the ability to stop the projector at any moment. Like Dorothy in the "Wizard of Oz", we can click our heels at any moment. Kansas awaits us and "there's no place like home".

Q) There seems to be a certain rhythm to our lives. How does it work? How does karma enter into this rhythm?

A) There is a sequential unfoldment to nature. There is a mathematics of unfoldment. There is a higher math of inter-action. Karma is just a product of permutations and combinations. The bad karmic numbers are out of sequence and retard unfoldment. The rates of entropy and unfoldment are prede-termined. Gods, Avatars, and Gurus can't change this plan. This is why it is so difficult to create a "Heaven on Earth". To accomplish a "Golden Age", everything from the finest sub-atomic particle to the size and shape of the universe would have to be slightly altered. The actual rules would have to change. Even if a God manifests on the Earth Plane, he is still bound be the rules of the sequence. He might have a lot of lat-itude, but when push comes to shove, he's got to play by the rules. That is why Avatars can't just go and Awakenen the world. At least this hasn't happened yet. To do so would immediately end the game and God loves a good game.

Q) Would you disclose a universal technique to bring me to Awakening.

A) Oneness Blessing!

Q) Do you have any advice to give us about how we should live our lives?

A) You have to live in your present moment mind. It is your authentic mind. To do this, you should not be so dependant on other people's advice. Their advice is not authentic because they are not you. They are not even themselves. It's your movie. Other people are living their own movie. Occasionally, there may be similarities. Most people's advice is simply a knee-jerk, socially imposed guess. No matter how well intentioned it may be, it is meant to control you. Other people cannot help you. After all, they have their own issues. They are unconscious too.

Become Self-referral. Become In-dependent. Become Self-ish. You have the power to choose anything, anytime. Your slavery is your choice. Your suffering is your choice. Your bondage is your choice. Your happiness is your choice. Your Awakening is your choice. There is nobody else to blame.

Q) Could you tell us a little about your new book?

A) These words that I have written are just a cover. They don't mean much in themselves. In fact, they are not significant at all. There are many great Sages who have expressed the truth of life with far greater eloquence. It is not the words; rather, it is the state that they will bring you to that is important. These words are a kind of gateway. There is a silence associated with them that is significant. If they are read, just know that you will gain a foothold in the area beyond your mind. You will come to know your Soul intimately. You will come to know your inmost Self. You will taste eternity. You will gradually awaken from a million lifetimes of sleep and you will know your Divinity. You will come to understand the wisdom of the Saints from time immemorial. This is why I was born. This is what I am here for. I am a gateway between Heaven and Earth. This gift is not in my personal control; rather, it is a Divine construct and I am humbled to carry it. To exist in this world, I have taken on a karma. I have a personal identity. I have children and grandchildren. I work hard and make many choices, as we all do. I have a past of actions, both good and bad, and I live the fruits of those actions. My life is action and action insulates the Divine. My life is both a protection as well as a challenge to overcome.

Q) Why is it so hard to change our habits?

A) I am a firm believer in the inflexible nature of reality. Thoughts are fixed. The cycle of our thoughts are fixed. The cycle of our thoughts represent a set of fixed physiologic nerve pathways. We are all locked into our own brain chemistry and it is always a self defeating cycle. The brain has to change. The pathways must be rerouted. Until the molecules reflect the universal mind.

Q) You sometimes refer to "Karmaland". What is it and how does it relate to the present moment?

A) This is Karmaland. It's another day on planet earth and we are immediately pulled into the madness. We step into the dream. We fully immerse ourselves and we are lost. Hours later, we awaken and are reborn to the present moment again. Where have we been? We have been in Karmaland. We have been accumulating karmas. Karmas are unconscious actions. Bad karmas are the result of sleepwalking through life. Good karmas, conversely, represent alert actions in the moment. In good karmas, we are awake to ourselves as we act. We are an alert witness and we are never lost, no matter how engrossing the activity.

Q) My mind seems to be moving all of the time. How does it process all of this information and who is observing the process?

A) Watch your eyes. They are constantly moving. All of your senses are moving. Your mind is moving as well. And how is all of this information being processed. It is happening one impulse at a time. Your mind may appear to be multi-tasking, but the data is actually being experienced by the mind in a very rapid sequential fashion. We are very binary. We are an on and an off. Life is just a myriad of impulses experienced one at a time. In the end, there is just the impulse and the observer: the Self.

Q) If we are God, why did we create this wild and ever-changing world? How does Awakening enter into the picture?

A) From the time that we first separated from the Self, millions of lifetimes ago, to the present moment, we have been unfolding our experience in the direction of Awakening. And what is Awakening? Awakening is just the re-identification with the Self. We have all bounced around like billiard balls for what seems like an eternity, just to end up back where we began. And why did we go through all of this? Well, we have to ask ourselves this question. When I ask, this is what I get. We basically got bored and we created this to flatter ourselves. Yes, we were once in a state of absolute perfection, but we chose Self-expression. We wanted to observe our own perfection and we are all presently engaged in glorifying that perfection. This process is taking place, simultaneously, on myriad levels, but we are normally only aware of this limited Earth Plane consciousness.

Q) Please talk about our eternal nature. What makes us eternal?

A) At birth, we in-corporate. Our Souls assume a physical body and the process of life begins. Until we die, until we un-incorporate again, breath goes in and out of our lungs, blood travels to the rhythmic beat of our hearts, and electrochemical impulses dance in our brains. We are living. Our mothers nourish us. Our parents clothe, house, and care for us. We burn matter. We burn other living matter. We assimilate life from other life. They become us and continue living through us. In time, we die. But we continue living after our physical death through our offspring. Using this perspective, we can say that we are as old as life and we will continue to live as long as there is life. The atoms which make up our bodies are as old as the universe and will continue to exist until the end of time. Although we are but a speck in the time line of eternity, we are great if we can recognize this eternal moment. The present moment is so great that it will outlive even time itself. In the moment, we were never born and we will never die. We are eternal, like God herself.

Q) What is the spiritual significance of the body?

A) The riddle cannot be solved. It is not enough to be spiritual. That alone will not move you. The solution transcends the mind. It cannot be observed. It is not a product of your life. The body is specially constructed for both transit and connection to the goal. It is our most valuable tool. Body is already Self-realized, but the mind-engendered karma maintains the illusion of bondage. Really, the body is the body of Nature.

Q) What is it like to live in the "Now".

A) If you live in the Now, you are your experience; your entire experience. There is no more fragmented reality. You are as much object as subject. You become unlocalized. You are in no space. You are in all spaces, simultaneously. The whole reality is so paradoxical. I try to explain this to people, but there are no takers. People ask me, "Why did you change your mind? Last week, last month, last year, you said such and such. Now you are saying the opposite. Which is it?" I reply to them. "It is both! They are not in conflict in my consciousness. There is room for every side." Now is the last vestige of what things were like before the Big Bang. What existed then, was no conflict, no duality, oneness, silence, fullness, no need to do anything, pre-creation, living in the womb, and an infinite latent potential. The Awakened live the Big Bang. They live right in the gap between matter and what existed before it. Pre-matter dominates their awareness. I am a big fan of the Oneness Blessing. If you are conscientious about receiving it, there is little further anyone can teach you. Oneness Blessing is fundamental to all paths.

Q) We are all so focused on success. We fear failure. How can we overcome this?

A) They are illusory. Both loss and gain are illusory. We are Divine Beings. We are uninvolved. We are One. We are really this moment only. You and I are only our present moment experience. Experience is just neutral. Experience is just what happens to us. But presently, we are asleep. We are too busy regretting the past or anticipating the future. God wants us to be awake. There is nothing else! Just be awake right now. What is, is Divine. Why live that which is not? It is not living. It is the dream. It is the source of all suffering. There is nothing to fear but being asleep. Be awake only. It is your birthright. No change in lifestyle is necessary to be awake because awake is not of this world. Awake is a different world. Awake is beyond any action. There are no pre-requisites. There are no philosophies, or secret techniques. An Awakened One can be a farmer, fireman or financier. These are of the world. They are of the body world. They comprise the world of breath, of mother, of flesh. But I am speaking of another world. It is our original home. It is perfectly still yet incredibly alive. We are all entitled to it. We are wired to experience all of the experiences of our normal everyday world as they play out on the screen of our Awakened world. Seek it in this moment. Be awake to it in this moment.

Q) How do we best reach the goal of Awakening?

A) There is nothing to do. There is nowhere to go. There is no doctrine to follow. There is no goal. There is no role. There is no point of view. There is nothing to achieve. There is no one to impress. Being is enough. But this is way too simple for most people. It takes a lot of Grace. It takes a lot of Grace to accept what is, on its own terms. Instead, we love the drama. We love the difficult, dangerous journey over hostile territory. And, unfortunately, the mind can never allow an end to the journey. Otherwise, it would be out of a job. In the Wizard of Oz, all Dorothy ever needed to do was just to click her heels; instead she chose an arduous and fearsome journey through Oz. You are also living in Oz. All you need to do is just click your heels.

Q) What is wisdom?

A) Wisdom is to know without thinking. It is knowingness. Wisdom does not involve the intellect. No sequential, logical analysis is involved. Wisdom is immediate knowledge. It is unequivocal knowledge. Wisdom is not relative. By this, I mean that it is knowledge untainted by doubt. There is absolutely no second guessing. All of the computers in the world hooked together could not render a more accurate solution. That is the wisdom of wisdom.

Q) Is there a difference between knowledge and wisdom?

A) Christ said, "You must be innocent like a child to enter the gates of heaven." It is the supreme truth. If you find yourself accumulating layer after layer of knowledge; just know that each layer pushes you further from the gates of heaven and each layer will eventually have to be eliminated. This is because knowledge is the opposite of wisdom. Wisdom is non-verbal. It is objectless and immediate and it has nothing to do with the world. True knowledge resides in the heart, not the head.

Q) What is the answer to life?

A) If I told you that I had the answer to life, you would probably laugh at me. If I told you that you had your own answer, you would probably laugh harder. But I'm serious. You have your own solution. After all, it is your puzzle. You know intuitively how you got here. Divine Grace will help you to get back out.

Q) What is the difference between a new soul and an old soul?

A) Old souls understand. They are bored with dreaming. You can recognize them. They are the ones who are driven to do whatever it takes to wake up. Wake up! You must do whatever it takes. Find Grace. Never be out of the Presence. The Presence will show you how never to leave, how never to drift away ever again.

Q) What is the nature of our behavior? Who is actually acting?

A) Behavior is an overlay. The Soul is uninvolved. To act

is just that. It's an act. Why is it an act? Action has no author. What is acting? Creation, maintenance and destruction are interacting upon themselves. The momentum for these actions comes from our personal past as well as from Cosmic forces which are responsible for the cohesive interaction of all objects in the Universe; including our thoughts and feelings.

Q) What is change? Is there anything permanent?

A) The nature of nature is change. Change is growth. Change reminds us of life's impermanence. It is impossible to imagine exactly how our lives will change. To know how our lives will change would not help anyway. To know would just change the changes into other changes. Nothing can be permanently changed because no change is permanent. Only the changing nature of change can be permanent. But this could change.

Q) What is the nature of the relationship between teacher and student?

A) There is a transmission of light between teacher and student. This light can only be passed of the student is open, opened at the heart. Student must be humble. That is why in India, the tradition is to bow to the teacher. When one bows to the teacher, one is bowing to their own infinite Self expressed as the teacher. When you bow, your crown chakra is aimed at the teacher's third eye. This is the perfect circumstance for the transmission of knowledge. Gurus don't let you know what they are doing. They heal you, help you avoid catastrophe, settle your enormous karmic debts, and help you to liberation with just a glance. Gurus never, ever display their power. It is all done naturally, invisibly.

Q) Why do we all have such strong opinions?

A) We all come into this life with notions of what is

important to us. We have all made choices before our birth to believe in certain principles to the exclusion of all others. We are all rigidly attached to our points of view. This is old. A lot of it is based on family tendencies. A lot is genetically based. Just understand that you believe what you believe because you are wired that way. For example, if an individual whose family has been practitioners of Islam for generations is taught to meditate using a Sanskrit mantra, chances are the individual will not have a good experience. Why? Genetics is the answer. Islamic nervous systems are wired differently form Hindu nervous systems.

Q) What is the relationship of the body to the Now?

A) I am fully awake. I know truth. It is a direct experience. It is not subject to mind. My body knows even before my mind. The body is the ancient one. I listen to it very carefully. This is because the mind can never be in the Now, while the body is essential to it.

Q) What are the limitations of language? What is the relationship of language to experience?

A) Last night, I was reading the "Crest Jewel of Discrimination" by Shankara. It struck me that these beautiful verses do not begin to put across the actual experience that Lord Shankara was attempting to convey. The best that language can do is to convey a notion. Language, itself, cannot transmit experience. Experience is always in the Now. Experience is always out of the pervue of the mind. But the experience of "the one without a second" that Shankara was describing was so powerful that even the fixed, frozen, nature of the English translation could not suppress the brilliance of Shankara's Knowledge. This is because the power of the experience poured through the gaps between the words, i.e., the power penetrated the silent spaces between the noises.

Q) If words and language are unable to convey experience, why are you writing a book?

A) This is a great question! My answer is that language can be used as a tool to transcend itself. That is the intention of this book. It is not just my personal intention. Rather, it is Divine in origin.

Q) Can you tell us about your spiritual tradition?

A) Grace is my supreme Guru. No earthly Guru has as much power to transform. Grace blends so seamlessly into itself. That is the source of its power. Grace creates invisibly. I know who I am. I know my role in this world but I do not share it with anyone. It would only serve to confuse. The tradition I represent is very ancient. Through it, change is created invisibly. No effort is involved. No technique is employed. Just Grace is employed! Just the natural, seamless power of Divine Grace is utilized.

Q) Can we get to Awakening through thinking?

A) We are awakened only when we get to the point where we stop asking questions. Wisdom begins where questions end. When we stop asking, we start living. Thinking is self-hypnosis. Thinking creates the dream. There is just no good thought. Only the silence in the gaps between the thoughts is of value.

Q) Can you tell us a little more about your personal experience?

A) I live beyond the pair of opposites. Life, as we commonly know it, does not operate the same way here. Laws are more fluid. For instance, a desire and its manifestation can actually occur in reverse order here. Manifestation is achieved without any logic. Intent is all it takes. Reality becomes just another dream. The witness, the Soul, is always in the same frame of reference. There is just the witness as separate from activity. There is no involvement in the field of action.

This is not just talk. This is a direct experience. It occurs within me. It is not a question of coming or going. Mind comes and goes. I remain eternally present. I am beyond mind. You are too. Just realize it. To realize it is a psycho-physiologic response. It is not just mental. Thought has a physical component. Both are necessary. Nerves must become stress-free. This process is gradual. Purification is not logical. Various things will happen at various points. What is toxic at one point may be incredibly beneficial at another. The Self unfolds itself, to itself, by itself. It knows precisely what is necessary for growth at any given moment. No system or book or teacher is capable of this. This is God's realm. It is the realm of Grace.

Q) Do the Awakened make choices through thinking?

A) The Awakened Ones are guided by a non-verbal intelligence. More accurately, a non-verbal intelligence taps into the Awakened. This intelligence is located in the Universal Soul. The Universal Soul contains the Creator's program for existence, from pre-existence to post-existence. The Awakened are entrained to this plan. The Awakened are assimilated into the Divine and what remains is a sequence of Divine impulses in human form. The Awakened do not move through personal choice. They are moved. A Divine Presence moves them. This Presence is all powerful. When we interact with the Awakened, we are actually interacting with the Divine Presence.

Q) Who are you? I mean, really, who is Stu Mooney?

A) I sit in this blinding light. I know. I just know. It is because this light is brimming with intelligence. This light hums and crackles with knowledge. But, it is expressed through me. It is being expressed through this body/mind.

This body/mind that you see in front of you just knows. Stu is karma. It is the localized expression of the universal knower as it is expressed thru Stu. It is Universal Stuness. Stu will continue to do what he was born to do. He will continue Stuing. He will act in this world like everyone else. Just allow the Divinity that Stu carries to shine through for you.

Q) Why are you reluctant to go deeper into the discussion of the experience of Awakening?

A) There is just no frame of reference for anyone to understand this process. It is the thoughts that tend to confuse them. People do not feel at home anywhere. There is so much doubt. There is no consistency to their experience. The Awakened know this. They keep to themselves. It is the only safe way. It will go on forever. Rocks will turn into plants. Plants will evolve into animals, and on and on to human bodies and then to bodies made of light. There is just no end. There is only absolute activity. There is only absolute silence.

Q) What is your present experience today? (12/21/2005)

A) My experience can be characterized as a letting go. One just wants to be in the experience. The world becomes peripheral. Moving matter, which was the hallmark of the previous state, does not make sense anymore. Letting things be is prominent now. It is more passive in nature. Yet, it is intrinsically more active. The experience is just so brilliant that nothing else can hold a candle to it. It is very, very intense. It is too deep and too powerful. There is a definite math to the experience. There is dimensionality. There is a sequential, geometric progression. It not only visual, it is also tactile. I feel patterns radiating from my skin. They seem to vibrate. I suspect the vibrating has to be a frequency that gradually loosens the sheath that covers the third eye. A cool minty wind now rises above the third eye. And a ringing in the ears is actively moving from ear to ear. Flashes of blue light abound every-where. Entertaining even a syllable of a mantra produces an overwhelming wavelike sensation which seems to radiate off into space. The mind remains perfectly clear through it all. There is a constant electric spark-like sensations moving up from the base of the spine. There is also pressure, circular movement and light emanating from the third eye. Third eye is now experienced as a tube of light that extends off into space and internally deep into the brain cavity, into the midbrain. In the previous state, I felt a direct connection with nature. I felt that I could directly influence what happens by my intention. This state is different. I am now too much in love to intend. It is as though intention would now create an artificial separation from the object. The crown chakra has become very active. There is tingling and movement all the time. There is now a link between sensation in the third eye and sensation in the crown. For instance, if I put attention in the crown, the third eye vibrates like crazy. Hands now tingle and twitch. My aura has become very clear and bright. Waves of light now protrude from my fingertips. It is beautiful to look at. All photos of holy people have become 3 dimensional. Faces have come out of the pictures. Faces also seem to move somewhat. In the previous state, all objects were perfectly distinct from each other. Each contained its own autonomous value. What was, simply was. All was black and white. This state contains these qualities but it is as if someone lubricated the gaps between the objects so that the distinction between them has softened. Unity is more predominant. The Creator lives close to this state. That is the reason for the intense ecstasy. I am feeling the Creator's love for us.

Q) What Is Awakening?

A) Awakening is the most overused word in spirituality. Awakening is just a symbol for something inexpressible. When I use the words enlightenment, liberation, awakening, and so on, it is done out of utter frustration. Perhaps it would have been better to use blank spaces where these words should go because it would mean exactly the same thing. NOTHING! Awakening is beyond our ability to conceptualize. That is why the Buddha would not even discuss the experience. But, for now, I will reluctantly bow to the requirements of language and grammar.

Q) What is Awakening?

A) In Awakening, everything moving stops. There is no more movement in the mind. Only the deepest silence exists. The people and all of the activities of the world are still there. But in the immensely rich silence, life becomes child's play. Every action, from the beginning of time till the end of time, and beyond, is now consciously available. There are no more secrets. The cosmic purpose of each moment is seen clearly.

Q) What is Awakening? What is ignorance?

A) Awakening is seamless. It is the perfect fit to what is, already. No one will ever be able to distinguish between ignorance and Awakening. Why? It is because the two states are identical in the relative sense. Then, what is the difference. The difference is indescribable. There is no frame of reference with which to evaluate Awakening. Awakening is the product of Grace.

I experience this state without strain but I could not convey it to you. I know if I tried to explain it to you, you would think it to death. Think of it this way. Awakening simply means more light. Life lights up. Life clears up. All events are now viewed in a cosmic context. It is so holistic. One may still react to life events intensely, but it is impossible, I repeat, it is utterly impossible to be lost in the events. You are never lost to your true nature. Your cosmic status shines through eternally. Even in deepest sleep one remains awake.

Q) What is Awakening?

A) Awakening is the pivotal concept. Awakening is the validation of life. It is the only experience we will ever have that is not subject to entropy. It is the payoff for the endless struggle of enumerable lifetimes. But Awakening is nothing like what we are led to believe by the spiritual community. I empathize with them. Language is the problem. Language is frozen. Language creates boundaries. And all of these boundaries are floating in blank empty space. All language, all relative knowledge, is inherently flawed because of this. Language is dead.

I live in a wordless awareness. I am awake to a reality which is devoid of knowledge. But, at the same time, it is filled with knowingness. I know knowing. I am knowingness, yet I am without knower, known, or the process of knowing. I am a state where enigmas, paradoxes, and contradictions all live harmoniously with each other.

Q) What is Awakening?

A) On a very deep level, you have answered the ultimate question. It's Awakening. You are becoming it. Even the body, its very cell structure is being transformed. A powerful process is now causing you to implode into your own being. It's a domino effect. The attention is gradually being drawn within. Nothing is lost. You are simply being sucked inside. The outside world loses its importance. Life becomes more casual. No big ups and downs. It is lived. Just let it do its thing. People are creatures of habit. They will do what they want. If they chose to come my way so be it. It is Grace. They are attracted by no pressure. Just roll with it and stay away from drama.

Q) What is Awakening?

A) Awakening requires a body and a mind. Awakening is localized. It is a uniquely Earth Plane phenomena. Awakening is really Awakening of the senses. Awakening is bringing light to all of experience. Awakening is Self-evident existence. It knows only Itself. Every breath, thought, action, and consequence of action is perfect. All becomes sacred. One becomes uninvolved without being separate. "This is my Light. This is my Matter. This is my Heart. This is all Me. I am Fullness".

Q) Can the Awakened change destinies?

A) Awakening changes destinies. The expression of natural law which permeates the air around the Awakened changes lives invisibly. It produces Awakened coherence. There is absolutely no doubt in the Awakened. There are no regrets. Every action fulfills the need of that moment, perfectly.

Q) What is Awakening?

A) Awakening is the sum total of one's experience in any given moment. Awakening is the unbounded process of experience. Thoughts and feelings are an aspect of this experience. In Awakening, ecstasy and pain can be experienced simultaneously. There is no limiting of experiential input. There are no gates. Data is perceived in raw form. It can be joyous. It can be painful. No matter what, it will be complete. And because it's complete, it will end completely. No residue will remain. The body/mind ceases to be a limiting factor. I am as much the sky, a cup, or my physical body. It is an interchangeable experience. There is just an eternal exchange of matter and energy. And time mediates the process.

Again, my definition of Awakening is being awake to the sum total of all of your experiences in a given moment. Now the mix of the total experience can and will change but the sum is always fixed. The sum total cannot be more or less than complete. Now is a deathless experience because it is greater than the sum of any of its parts. Even if you were murdered in this moment, that last moment exists only as a tiny aspect, a constituent part of the now. The Now remains unaffected by it. Now is not a product of the Earth Plane. It is located at the doorway between your mind and your Soul.

Q) What is Awakening?

A) If we could just bear to listen to ourselves, there would be no questions. The Awakened listen so carefully. All the information is there. In silence, in each moment, it is revealed effortlessly. We all know it. We know it all. We just don't want to risk pain so we cover it over. Knowledge is complete knowledge. It is the full range of possibilities. Nothing is excluded. After all, life is just a set of experiences based on our past karmas. Even after Awakening, it still comes. Sometimes, it comes even more than before because it all has to play out in just one lifetime. Then, we can finally return home.

Q) What is Awakening?

A) Awakening is s strange experience. Being awake in a world that is asleep is strange. It is lonely too. There is a lot I can't say. It would only serve to confuse. The confusion stems from our habit of using the lower self rather than the higher self to function in the world. Literally, everything you experience, I experience the opposite. Black for you is white for me and vice versa. So it may seem that I am always trying to disagree or to challenge people's realities but it is based on my frame of reference. You see, I am inside out.

Q) What is Awakening?

A) I want to tell you the most important thing. Awakening is not of this world. It has nothing to do with what is happening to you right now. Nothing will change when it happens. Only you will change. Your point of reference will change. You will be emancipated. You will think, "Oh yes, I am awake!" You will immediately understand the deal. Awakening is internal. No one will know unless you tell them. Even then, they won't believe you because they only know this world. They think that Awakening means that one's world has to change. No! I am telling you the truth. Awakening is not of this world. If you are looking for change in this world; Awakening is not your ticket. Change in this world involves doing. Awakening is completely uninvolved. Nothing that you presently know has the slightest thing to do with it. Do you want to know why? It is because you believe that there is a localized you that is reading this. There isn't. There is just the experience of reading. That's it!

Q) What is Awakening?

A) Awakening is the final process in nature's evolutionary expression. Nature pushes everything in creation towards this one goal because it is the crowning achievement; the end game. Unfortunately all of creation works against it as well. Everything distracts us from enlightenment. Everything in creation is driven relentlessly towards it yet this very move-ment draws our attention away from it. We get so distracted by everything that we miss the one thing that underlies every-thing. And that is really nothing.

Q) How do I get Awakened?

A) How do you get here? And where is here? Grace has to happen. Grace has to cause an infinite number of variables to line up perfectly. It has to be a perfect roll of the dice. Literally, every molecule of every DNA strand of every cell in the body has to line up in such a way as to play nature's song flawlessly. In India, they call this song the Ved. It means knowledge of life.

Q) Why are the Awakened so secretive?

A) I can understand why these holy people crave privacy.

The whole civilized world looks completely insane. People run and run without stopping. Life after life they run after something they can never really possess. I love them all.

Q) What is the role of the Awakened?

A) The role of an Awakened One is very simple. It is to radiate Divine Light on to the Earth Plane. There is no other purpose to be in a body after the Awakening. One is Awake in a body only to provide a vehicle for God's work. One's individual role has forever changed. When an Awakened One meditates, it is only to bless the Earth Plane. There is work to perform. The work gets performed through the Awakened. The Earth is graced by the Awakened without their involvement. Service is the only thing in their awareness.

Awakened Ones shun the spotlight for the most part. They do not wish to deal with ignorance. They know Truth. A few worthy students may come along. They are attended to, but that's it! The world is simply left to itself.

Q) What is Awakening?

A) Awakened beings control without controlling. They will let you run and run and run without any fear of losing you. Why? It is because you are unconsciously operating within their consciousness. You can never be outside an Awakened beings experience. They are you. They are the embodiment of your Soul.

Q) What is the relationship of the Awakened to God?

A) God has an agenda. Those who are identified with the Self execute this agenda. Sometimes it is not pretty but it must be done. The Awakened are given a choice to stay in this world of uncertainty or go back into the silent source.

Q) Is Awakening physical?

A) Awakening is an organic process. Awakening is perfectly functioning brain chemistry. Awakening is our natural state. Our species is currently functioning at a sub-normal, sub-human level. All of the right chemicals are there but they are out of order. Awakened functioning refers to the correct sequencing of our brain chemistry. You know, there is really no world out there because we experience the out there from in here; ie, inside the brain. In other words, the brain interprets and creates our world for us. So, it would follow, that when we are correctly sequenced, we would be able to interpret the "out there" more accurately. Correct interpretation of the "out there" would lead to action in harmony with Natural Law. We would, then, experience the support of Nature for all of our actions because we would have become just a reflection of Nature's sequential unfoldment.

Q) Is Awakening physical?

A) Consciousness and Chemistry are one. We experience through our chemistry. Awakening is just a product of the right molecules in the right order. It is like the combination to a safe. One just has to have the right molecules attached to the right receptor sites and that's it. The door swings open and we have full access to the riches within. I am hopeful of a more scientific approach to evolution. The path of Yoga is an ancient technology. It produces success, but in very limited numbers. We need a radically transformative tool. We need a new Veda. We need a new Universal blueprint for the rapid development of the Nervous System. Oneness Blessing is the best solution that I have encountered for the development of an Awakened chemistry.

Q) What is Awakened action?

A) An Awakened person is capable of any possible behavior at any moment. It is impossible for such a being to make a mistake in an absolute sense. The behavior may seem socially inappropriate, but, it is absolutely perfect. This is difficult for most of us to understand. How can socially inappropriate behaviors be perfect? It is because an Awakened being is completely natural. An Awakened being is so natural that there is no difference between Awakened action and Natural Law itself. In other words, An Awakened being would find it impossible to entertain an "unnatural thought". Awakened action simply fulfills the need of the moment.

Q) What is Awakening?

A) There are Souls among us who are awake to themselves. They are their own eternity. They live life as they choose. We are attracted to the great lights, the great teachers; like Yogananda, Shankara, Ramana Maharishi, and Ramakrishna to name but a few. But these are a minority of the Awakened. This Earth Plane owes its very existence to the invisible ones. They walk among us and we hardly notice. But we are breathing their breath and we could not exist for a moment without their awareness. They are the Self-revealed existence. They are the Self of all. They are Divine and only guests here. The Invisible Ones blend in so perfectly that they are inseparable from that which is not. It is both their great gift and also their burden.

Q) Why should I get Awakened?

A) The answer is as clear cut as Heaven or Hell. I swear that it is that dramatic a difference. You are in Hell right now and you need desperately to wake up from the dream. The funny thing is, you don't even know that it is Hell and you will defend it to the death the moment anyone challenges your reality. That is why Awakened Ones shun society. Why bother?

Q) Most religions incorporate light into their worship of the Divine. What is the significance of light?

A) Only light heals. Light is the source of matter. All matter is struggling to become light again. Humans are the transitional form between matter and light. Light is intelligence. The highest intelligence is the greatest light. That is why it is called enlightenment. Light has finally healed all ignorance and no darkness remains. The physical body has a hard time with light. For example, too much sunlight can damage the skin. The physical body can be transformed to light only gradually and with greatest care.

Q) Why does our life feel complete even before we are Awakened?

A) It is because all levels of Consciousness are experienced as complete unto themselves. The Vedas state, "Knowledge is structured in Consciousness". This is the most fundamental concept. Our understanding is relative to our ability to experience the object of perception and understanding or knowledge of the object will be different in different states of Consciousness. Therefore, "Knowledge is structured in Consciousness" is another way of saying that every one of us lives in a completely unique world.

Q) Can you speak to us about the nature of time?

A) I can't waste time on what I never had. I am out of time. I feel timeless. I haven't a moment to spare. My time is up. Even the tick of the clock seems to take forever. Actually, it takes even longer than that but I don't have the time to explain. So I'll get back to you some other time about it. I wish that you could synchronize your time with my time. It would only take you a single moment to do. Just live in this single moment all the time and we will be in synch with each other forever.

Q) What is the significance of the Sun?

A) We are all just the sun in different disguises. We originated in the sun. Somehow, the sun contained the blueprint for life. The sun is the origin of all physical manifestation. The sun is also the source of the mind. The sun is the source of subject and object. The sun is the source of cause and effect. The sun is the source of all miracles beginning with life; the primordial miracle. The brilliant light of the sun is the closest we can ever physically get to experience the light of God. That is why most great religions worship the sun.

Q) Can you speak to us more about the "Web".

A) Every object is brimming with intelligence. It is easy to sit here and look at anything, even at nothing, and be able to go deep into the essence of the object. At the finest levels, all objects are inextricably linked in space time. I have earlier, referred to this link as the web: the space/time continuum. The web is the creator's program like a computer operating system. The web is the intelligence between objects. Intelligence is the relationship of one object to another. The web is only available when one is perfectly still. Only then does the connectivity between all objects become apparent. One then is able to sit in the home of all intelligence as a silent witness.

Q) Is it hard for you to operate in this world anymore?

A) I see everything exactly opposite from "normal" consciousness. Understanding has flipped 180 degrees. Everything, even the slightest thing, becomes so important that no single thing seems more important than any other thing. Each moment is completely full. There is no downtime. Even doing nothing is filled with everything. And that is something to think about, only, thinking about it is still no more important than any other thing.

Q) Can you speak about healing? How does it work?

A) Healing is the product of a silent mind. Health is silence and light. When everything moves except you, you are ready to heal others. Touch heals and silent touch can transform. But sight healing, healing by looking into another's eyes, is the most powerful. Sight healing requires a perfectly silent mind. One can see into the other's Soul. Their Soul will entrain to your silence and their karmas can then be dissolved.

Q) How can we help suffering humanity?

A) The only solution is a quantum shift in consciousness. The miraculous must become a way of life. Grace matters. That's the nature of Awakening. A gaping hole in consciousness opens up and Grace pours in. We awaken. Then one lives in the gap between matter and time. The Awakened existence is virtual. It is matter/non-matter. The Awakened become a living paradox. They become an enigma. Awakened Ones exist but they really shouldn't. It is Grace which keeps them localized. The Awakened Ones live eternity within boundaries.

Q) What if you don't like Awakening? Can you come back?

A) Once you've gone, you can never come back. You will never feel or look at anything "normally" again. Fun isn't fun after that point because you can never be fully involved in any activity ever again. You will be separate. You will be blissful but bliss is not good or bad. It is apart and qualityless. You will still feel everything. You will not be numb. You will feel fully and yet there will be a cushion of bliss. You will feel disengaged, at least partially, from your experience. You will never feel really "human" again because you will feel some sort of Divinity all of the time. You will no longer be measured by other men. Your job will have changed. In whatever you do, you will be doing God's work.

Q) Can we heal before we are healed?

A) If we heal another before we are completely silent, we will end up transferring our shake onto the people we are healing. They become corrupted by our shake. The less we shake, the more light we emit. Disease is the absence of light. Silence is the sound of light and healing is the by product of silence. Healing is the effortless restoration of light to the body/mind. We already inherently know we are light. A silent healer just reminds us of that. The truth is that we heal ourselves. Disease is just discordant light. A silent healer restores coherence to our light.

Q) What is the value of language?

A) Language is useful only to transcend language. Some day, we will fall into a gap between two thoughts that will never end. From this point, there is a natural process of accepting that we have, in fact, fallen into eternity. "I" no longer means the same thing. More and more, "I" stands for everything. Ego simply vanishes into a gigantic ocean of awareness. We lose the boundary of where "I" ends and the "other" starts. The other becomes as precious to me as my personal self. When we stop moving, then our life becomes real for the first time. Life's only a dream when we are dreaming. When we stop moving, we will begin feel the spin of the earth. We will feel Mother Earth' pulse. We will begin to experience the reality that we are all encased in this enormous womb which the Indians refer to as "Hiranya Garbha" or the Golden Egg and our primordial Mother is in gestation, just waiting to give birth to her children, who will all be Gods.

Q) Why is it so hard to transmit Awakening?

A) It is hard to even begin. You will forget. Why? You are in mind. Mind is in constant change. You may "get it" for a time but your mind cannot experience. An Awakened One may give you a higher states experience but your mind will label it and, by the next morning, it will sound vague. The night before, it seemed so real. But now it sounds like boring words. Why? Your mind has erased a glimpse of the non-mind.

Q) What is truth?

A) Truth is what is. But truth is structured in consciousness. My truth may not be yours. Natural law determines whether my truth resonates with your truth. If you hear me, then our destinies are parallel. We will serve natural law together.

Q) What is the nature of action? What is inaction?

A) There are laws. There are underlying principles governing action, all action. These principles exist in perfect silence. Action is governed by inaction. Those who live inaction control action. They know inaction to be brimming over with action. In fact, inaction is so active as to be almost uncontainable. Just an innocent thought in a state of inaction will produce virtually any result in the active field. This is the active expression of silence. It is wonderful to observe this active inaction. It is like watching God's archetypal blueprint for creation. Whatever you can imagine will happen. The grip of individuality has loosened. Life is now experienced from multiple points of view. It is more holistic. It engenders compassion. All sides now seem to validate one experience. Even the word "my" is seen in a broader context.

Q) Sometimes I feel like I will never get Awakened. Will it happen for me and what will it be like?

A) Some day, some where, some time, your mind will stop moving. Your center will no longer be your thoughts. Your center will be frozen in place. Life then passes through you while you remain motionless. You will still feel everything just as before. But now you will have a choice. You can honor a thought or disregard it. You are completely uninvolved. Your body/mind may still have the same proclivity for such things as heart trouble, ulcers, anxiety and the like. These are deep matter karma. They are the momentum of previous births being played out. But you are eternal and beyond these things because you are no longer identified with the body/mind.

Q) Does an Awakened man or woman have a "personal" life?

A) Awakening is a very special gift. One feels completely in the hands of God. It is as if God has loaned one out to the earth plane. It is as if God is using one's eyes, one's body, one's mind, to move through her creation. Still, the Awakened One has a personal life. But it seems to move to a beat, a rhythm, a dance which merges personal with impersonal. It's a huge wave. It is a huge wave of unfolding consciousness and the Awakened One has become the ultimate surfer. There is a momentum; a previous life energy. The Awakened one remains expressed as it. It is his existence, his cover. His individual way exists to express his infinity. People have a basic misunderstanding of Awakened Souls. We think that Awakened Ones are beyond human, superhuman. But superhuman, in this context, means supremely human, completely human, experiencing all levels at once. They experience the full range, all the way from the animal to the Divine. What is most important, in this state, is the experience itself, not the object of experience. It is carrying the innocence of a child into every moment. Awakened ones can speak to the humanity deep inside everyone. This is what gets beyond our masks. Awakening is an intensely intimate experience because there is nothing between oneself and the other person. One becomes God, deeply expressed in a human form. An Awakened One is infinitely weak because she defends against nothing. An Awakened Soul has the full range of his humanity available to himself at each moment. She is protecting nothing. The "normal" human lives in fear. And all fear is the fear of death. The Awakened Soul is Oneness. She knows it will never die. Because we are fearful, we only allow socially acceptable bits and pieces of out humanity to be available to others. We fear ridicule. When one is Awake, one is completely and perfectly oneself. One is no longer trying to fit oneself into a culturally imposed paradigm. In order to be Awakened, we have to be willing to become completely who we are, without any of the mystique. Then we will realize that we are absolutely the most beautiful creature that God ever created.

Q) Can I experience the Self? What is it like?

A) I am in the Self, I am pure experience. I am only the Universal mind. There is no localized identity. The personal mind vanishes like a raindrop in the ocean. The "I" assumes the qualities of the Soul. Obtain Oneness Blessing and you too will experience this.

Q) Your life seems very simple and uncomplicated. It seems boring. Is it?

A) My life is incredibly uncomplicated. It is utter simplicity. But, to others, it appears empty. This is because they are empty and constantly have to be filled or distracted. I am fullness. I cannot be any "more full".

Q) What is a Guru's job?

A) "I am my own world". A Guru's only job is to convince us of this. It is strange, but, in the end, our ego wins. Only, by the time that it wins, it has taken on an infinite, limitless dimension. So, ultimately, it wins and loses simultaneously. There is a point in deep meditation where we merge with the Pure Consciousness. It could be called the win/lose point. The ego wins but it becomes unlocalized. We have a winner but no one to give the trophy to. This win/lose point is the goal of all existence. It is the most fascinating experience to cross back and forth across this invisible boundary. It is like being born and dying over and over again. The real source of power comes from being FULLY CONSCIOUSNESS as we cross this boundary. We must become very familiar with this area. Everything that exists had to cross this win/lose point. In time, we gain knowledge of how nothing turns into something. We gain an understanding of how infinity congeals into a point. Fully conscious and fully awake, I can't stress this enough. At the beginning of our meditation experience, we pass this win/lose point but our nervous systems have so much stress and fatigue that we literally miss the point. Instead, we experience the transition through this point as a sort of blank spot in our meditation practice. It is almost impossible to transit this point or gap without God's intent for you to experience it.

Q) What is personal reality?

A) There are many realities co-existing in the present moment. Each reality comes with its own version of the truth. Each truth is valid for that particular reality. Therefore, it is invalid for any other reality.

This is why we are so attached to our own point of view. Our own truth is correct. Unfortunately, another's truth may be equally correct from the standpoint of their own reality. This is the seed of all misunderstanding.

Q) What is the nature of knowledge?

A) Knowledge is self evident and all knowledge is available everywhere. Why is this? Let's first look at knowledge. My definition is that knowledge is the relationship between the subject, the object, and the process linking the two together. Another way of saying this is that knowledge is the relationship between the knower, the known, and the process of knowing. Usually, there is an enormous gap between the subject and the object. The subject must work hard to know the object. The object seems elusive. That is because the subject is trying to understand the object outside the present moment. The mind is busy trying to understand the object by looking into the past in order to construct a future understanding of the object. The subject does not see that his own subjectivity influences his knowledge of the object. Now earlier I mentioned the knower, the known and the process of knowing. These three aspects have one source. They are actually aspects of a singular energy. These three aspects were one, self-evident, knowledge prior to breaking into subject, object and the link. So there is a singular energy which is a fourth value to knowledge. And it is awareness itself. We could call it pure consciousness. In India, it is sometimes referred to as the Samhita value or the source value of knower, known, and process of knowing. When we live in the present moment fully, the three values of knowledge merge into the fourth. No gap in understanding the object now exists because one is living the source of both the subject and the object. That is why I said in the beginning, that all knowledge is self evident and is completely anywhere. The key is to live the moment. This explains why I could write this book at my desk in a carpet store. You see, I didn't write it in a carpet store; I wrote it in the eternal now.

Q) Please talk to us about the "Now".

A) The "Now" is the sum total of all experiences in this moment. The "Now" can never be experienced by the mind because the mind and the "Now" are diametrically opposed. If you could spend a lot of time in the now (even though now has no time) you would come a long way. Your destiny would change. Now is the great connector. Now and Grace are one. Now and God are one. Now and Awakening are one.

Q) Can there be action in the "Now"?

A) Now is a state of action. That is, all actions exist only in the Now. The past and future contain no possibility of action. Action is occurring only in this moment. I am acting now. I am typing now. You will see the words on the page then, but you will be seeing only the fruits of action, not the actual act of typing. Action is. Action is not "was". Action is not "will be". Mind cannot exist in the Now, so the Now is beyond thought. Mind must exist first for thought to exist. Therefore, since Now is a state of action, and Now can contain no mind, then it would follow that action exits in a state separate the mind, separate from the thought. This is why it is so hard to manifest a thought. Thought can't exist in the field of action. Manifestation or the fruit of an action, is a Now experience. But the thought that precipitated the fruit of an action can never co-exits with the action. The answer to the problem of manifestation lies in finding the common source to both the Now and the Mind. The source of thought is that link. In the source of thought, or Ritam Bara Pragya, one experiences a thought and its manifestation simultaneously. This is because the source of thought is both the source of the individual mind as well as the source of the Now. It links the two in absolute silence.

Q) Does consciousness have a source?

A) There is a bottom to Consciousness. There is a source. This source is perfectly still. All movement ceases. It is deeply electric. It is vibrating nothingness. It is a field of dreams and its nature is magic. It is Oneness. It is the source of Natural Law. No intention is needed for manifestation here. This is because your mind and the mind of Nature become one. If you have a desire, just know that Nature is having it too. You are inseparable from the source now and things go smoothly in your life. Even the things you didn't know you needed just happen for you. You are on the fast track and life becomes very pleasant. There is nothing more to attach yourself to because you are already getting everything you need. Everyone who gets near you gets your light and times will be good for them as well.

Q) Shouldn't we control our desires?

A) If you react to trigger words like, sex or drugs, if you run from material success, then you need to be honest with yourself. You are running from these things because you fear your own desire for them. One way or another, you must get to a neutral point with these desires. You must face your desires. These are deep, primordial drives that have many lifetimes of momentum behind them. They are karmic seeds which must be roasted. There is absolutely no difference between attraction or aversion towards an object. They are both indicative of attachment. You can neutralize them through Oneness Blessing.

Q) Shouldn't we imitate the behavior of the Awakened?

A) Imitating the goal is not a path to gain the goal. Imitating the goal only creates another layer of ignorance to be burnt away. Nature operates in complete harmony and effortlessness. There is absolutely no control involved. Evolution must be invisible. Evolution is not a mood. It cannot occur through controlling of fixing the mind. Fixing the mind is a byproduct of Awakening.

People try to imitate Awakened people. For instance, people try to stop thoughts because Awakened people say they have no thoughts, no mind. The mind can never be used to kill the mind. When one realizes that all the knowledge of the mind comes from consciousness itself, then one realizes the possibility of living a life without the mind. The mind will still exist but it will be without boundaries, without limitation. It will not be localized in space and time. The mind can never be conquered on the level of the mind. This can only be achieved through the infusion of Grace. God must choose to Awaken you.

Those who try to imitate Awakening, create an imbalance within their nervous system. This is because nature has always evolved without the slightest effort. Human evolution is natural. The closer to nature we are, the closer to Awakening we are. Awakening is being one with Nature. We become Natural Law. There is a direct relationship between a completely ignorant and an enlightened person. Both are completely natural and comfortable with themselves. But everyone on the path is in between. They are neither ignorant nor Divine but somewhere in between.

Q) What is liberation?

A) Liberation is realization of the Soul. It is the pivotal experience. It separates the men from the boys. From this point, the soul gradually creeps into the senses, ego, mind and intellect. The subtle worlds become available. Finally, only the Soul remains. The body/mind and the world then become just a faint idea of the Soul.

Q) Can you talk to us about relationship?

A) Relationships are always relative because, by definition, more than one participant is involved. Therefore, there is more than one point of view in every relationship. The subject of one side of a relationship becomes the object to the other participants in a relationship. No two parties can ever have the same point of view. This is the crux of the problem. No one sees things the same way as the other person. Ever! This is the source of all relationship problems. So what is the solution to the problem of relationships? The solution to relationships is to personally experience Oneness. The Oneness within us is identical to the Oneness of the other participant in the relationship.

Q) Does the Universe influence the development of Awakening in the individual?

A) The Universe creates an Awakening within the individual. The Universe is constantly moving our nervous systems towards perfect orderliness. Perfect orderliness means perfect harmony with nature. There is a power inside of us which molds us on a very subtle level. As we develop, we become aware of very fine waves sweeping back and forth through the body's electrical field. This is God moving through us. These waves are programmed in us at our birth to recur throughout our lives at specific times and locations. They subtly work to bring us in harmony with the Universal Mind. The end product is One Mind, One Being; a perfect replica of the body of the Creator.

Q) Is the Earth the only intelligent world?

A) This is not the only world. Above the Crown Chakra, there are areas of more subtle light in the form of worlds much like our own. The higher above the Crown one goes, the finer and more pure are these worlds. There is life in the form of light beings, angels, Gods, and Goddesses. They are the stuff that dreams are made of.

Q) Can you describe Samadhi? Can you manifest desires from Samadhi?

A) Samadhi is a state of perfect silence. This world vanishes and the Soul remains. Nothing is left. The state of the Soul is a state of no movement. There are no qualities; no subject; no object; no relationship. No desire can be entertained here. Manifestation does not occur within Samadhi. Manifestation requires desire. Manifestation requires the relationship of subject to object over time. Gurus manifest within the sphere of matter and change. They manifest from a spot where the Soul turns to matter. Where does the Soul end? The Soul ends in a wave. This wave identifies the boundary between the Soul and the Non-Soul. The wave has a definite quality. It is a sound wave. The sound of the wave is the sound "Ah". Within "Ah" are 51 sub-tones which serve as the building blocks for matter and for thought. So the source of our thoughts is our own Soul. Thoughts are unmanifest God within the Soul. Thoughts become manifest in wave form as the "Ah" wave, a sort of membrane, gets penetrated. The Soul gets localized as the "Ah" wave and then gets fragmented further into the 51 sub-sounds .These sub-sounds are like the building blocks of our world. Internally, they become thoughts. Externally, they become matter. The key to manifestation is to understand the relationship between thoughts and matter. Matter becomes linked to thought at the point of the "Ah" wave. Gurus take their awareness to this point and manipulate thought to create matter.

Q) I have been with a Guru for 15 years. He is wonderful but I am not sure I am growing. What should I do?

A) I met a guy this morning. He told me that he had a Sufi master. He had practiced with his master for more than 30 years. This individual had been to many, many retreats and he was about to return to India once again to study. But it was obvious to me that the goal, Awakening, was no longer considered possible by him. Instead, the technique, the tradition of Masters, and all of the other trapping of the path had replaced the goal. I see this often and it is very sad. Why do this? What's the point? The point was never the path. The point is the goal. Awakening is the only point. All the rest is just bondage. Now the teacher may be very nice. He/she may be charming, fascinating and mysterious. But that's not the goal, is it? The teacher is not the goal. You have to step back with a cold neutral vision and see what is. Don't rationalize or try to overlook inequities. What is, is! Get the lead out and do something to facilitate your growth right now. Don't allow yourself to get dull or sad. So many devotees think that the goal is about suffering. They believe that evolution is the product of control and discomfort. This is wrong! The goal, True Awakening, is not involved at all with action. Therefore, no specific set of actions will ever predispose you to awakening. One has ABSOLUTELY NOTHING to do with the other. So practicing all of the austerities on the planet will never do a thing to help you. Divine intervention is the only refuge.

Q) Is there ever a point where my world will stop changing?

A) There are two worlds. One changes and one does not. There is no connection between the two. The non-changing world underlies the changing one. But there is no link. There is no crossover. So the ever changing world can only change within itself. Everything about the changing world is temporal and in motion. We all normally live the ever changing world. Everything that we experience from our first breath, reinforces the unstable nature of life. Then, one day, through Divine Grace, our mind will finally stop moving. It is an experience completely beyond description. In a flash, the ever changing becomes the never changing. And for the first time in our lives, there is real stability and silence. Our mind isn't all over the place anymore. It becomes frozen in just one point of view and it stays there permanently. One becomes like a Sun which never sets.

Q) How do I know that I am God?

A) We have to look around and see that this is all us. Now, we may look like a phone, a door, a rock, the smell of a rose or a soft touch, but it is us, nonetheless. These things are as much us as our own physical body. We are really just flowing, motion-filled, creation. We spin and roll as God. We are the substance of everything, everywhere. When we truly realize this, our lives will be forever changed. We will become Cosmic. We will realize that the localized self is just a tiny aspect of us. We can't be hurt. We can't be limited in any way. All of these colors, textures, emotions, everywhere are indeed an expression of our own Self. Just be conscious. That's all.

Q) Can holy people be "Normal"?

A) There are not a lot of "Normal" holy people. Their reality is not available to us. Holy people tread a dangerous line. This world is logic bound. They may be here with us, but holy people have a limitless freedom at their basis. Their experience is, literally, 180 degrees from our own. So it is hard for them to play our tune because they are also busy dancing to the beat of the Creator.

Q) "I am the Universe". What does this really mean?

A) First, we must distinguish between the thought of being the Universe and the actual experience of being Universal. Thoughts are the symbols of experience and it turns out that experience is actually not of the mind. Experience is of the witness. Only the Soul can experience. "I am the Universe", is the direct experience of the Soul's true nature. This world is just recycled Soul. The physical body has to be cultured to withstand the Universal experience. The physical body, by its very nature, is localized. Non-local experience is very difficult for the body/mind to process. The body does not feel "held together" during the non-local experience. The body tends to panic (a very blissful panic). Unity Consciousness happens in the world. It is a physical body phenomenon. Unity is the ultimate sense experience. One becomes both sense and non-sense (while remaining senseless).

Q) What is Unity Consciousness?

A) To truly live the eternal moment is to actually become eternal and unlimited. It is the most advanced state of Awakening. It is Unity Consciousness. Unity is a Supramental, Superhuman state. In Unity, one vibrates at light speed. Unity is a state of overwhelming Oneness.

Q) Is there really a heaven? What is it like?

A) I love the popular notion of heaven. Heaven is thought to be a place where there is no pain. It is said to be a place of eternal happiness and joy. I want to set the record straight about heaven. Heaven has nothing to do with pleasure and pain or good and evil. Heaven is about bliss. And bliss is an indefinable experience. Bliss is beyond all pairs of opposites. Bliss is beyond mind, thought or understanding. Bliss is a perfectly pure ecstasy and can be lived in the here and now. Learn to live the bliss of heaven right now.

Q) Can the mind know the Self?

A) Mind is the Soul's vehicle to know itself but the mind can never completely know the knower. All of our thoughts, actions and experiences add up to the same totality of experience in every moment of our lives. The moments may all be different, but the total quantity of experience in each and every moment is always the same finite amount. The quantity and quality of our thoughts, emotions, and sense experiences are constantly in flux. But these variables change directly in proportion to each other so that the sum total of experience is always the same. Now is the sum total of experience. Experience it NOW!

Q) Why do some Gurus seem to allow their bodies to deteriorate?

A) Once the Third Eye opens, nothing is really necessary

for growth. The process will continue to unfold towards its goal of complete fulfillment. The main concern is to keep the body going. This is because the higher experiences take place in very fine levels of awareness. Most of higher living takes place in a realm beyond thought. It is an area of just tiny, tiny impulses. It's just an area of glorified nothingness. This is far, far away from the gross physical body. Therefore, it is an effort to stay connected to the physical. In other words, it is easy to ignore the physical and let the body fall into disrepair. Edgar Cayce is a good example of a developed soul who neglected the physical.

Q) We all seem to react to things as if we are programmed. Is this true? Do we really have a choice in what we do?

A) On any given day, we act from a program which exists within our Soul. Actually, this program is located just above our Soul, in the area of our intellect. We are like billiard balls. Our Soul-based program causes us to continually interact with every atom in the entire universe. Our programmed actions, which occur in perfect harmony and in perfect sequence, eventually bounce back to their origin and affect their originator. This is the law of Karma. Our Karma is unavoidable because we are, in a sense, condemned to live out our program. Choice, then, is not really a choice. Choice is just part of the original program. Now, in extreme cases, our program can be overridden. Buddha, through Divine Grace and intense moment awareness, overrode his program. He was born to be a prince but, through pure unbroken attention, he made himself into a Buddha; an Awakened One.

Today, Think to yourself the following: I am the goal. I override my present circumstance; my program. I tap into the energy of Divine Grace and through attention only, I change my role. I utilize the energy of the Infinite moment. This moment transcends time. It is the time of the Creator before his Creation. I am forever this Holy moment. I am a holy man in this holy moment.

Q) How do I know when I am Awakened? What is it like?

A) I am complete. There is no object of desire outside of my own consciousness. There is no longer a need to be more. More is already within me. I am free. I am my own self-referral consciousness.

For this consciousness to exist, all notions must die. The slate must be clean. It is impossible to achieve without Divine Grace. Nothing, no Guru, no liberation, no hopefulness, no emptiness, nothing can be left. This is so difficult because the mind is such a deceiver. YOU CANNOT TRUST YOUR OWN EXPERIENCE BECAUSE YOUR MIND CAN IMITATE LIBERATION. Since this is the case, it is possible that you could end up with what I call a "conceptual liberation". Conceptual liberation is a subtle overlay over the Self. In India, this state is sometimes referred to as "Bhava Samadhi" or, literally, false samadhi. Only Divine Grace can see it and wipe it out.

Q) What does it take to get Awakened?

A) It takes Divine intervention to grow. Grace must be the goal. Only Grace creates liberation. There are some key factors in growth. One should be consistent in spiritual practice. One should practice what one believes in. No gaps. Like clockwork, it should be practiced daily. Loving attention is best. One must be undistracted. So kill your dramas.

Q) What is the value of the Third Eye? What is it like when it opens?

A) Let's talk about the Third Eye. When it opens, it is like we are living inside a jewel. All sense perception becomes greatly enhanced. Light breaks into spectral-colored facets. It is like living inside a beautifully cut ruby. It is a very soft, electric experience. The experience is brimming with intelligence. After the Third Eye opens, creation comes alive. We can feel the presence of the breath of the Creator everywhere. One feels it underlying and animating everything. There is an area high up in the nasal passages that opens with the opening of the Third Eye. Prana then goes to the higher areas of the Limbic System and Pituitary Gland in the brain and to the Sahasrahra or crown in the subtle body. When the Third Eye opens, the energy which used to go to the two physical eyes gets channeled upward to the area between the eyebrows. The physical eyes, in a sense, go blind. Then we begin to see everything through the Third Eye. Note: Do not try to activate the Third Eye on your own. It is an extremely delicate instrument. Force can damage it. This damage can be irreversible in this lifetime. What opens the Third Eye? Grace does. This opening is the culmination of lifetimes of conscientious attention to spiritual practice. Much guidance from many holy persons went into the opening. There are no freak accidents. Grace comes from the Creator. There are no shortcuts.

After the Third Eye opens, we are never the same. Our old world is permanently overthrown. This experience is so extraordinarily beautiful that there is nothing else in life that can hold a candle to it. It is the most addictive experience that one could ever image. One taste, and we are hooked for life. That is why saints all over the world have written volumes about the experience and all religions have their foundations in it. Buddha left his family and his kingdom for it. Christ died for it. Think about it. It must be pretty special. Although opening the Third Eye is not the same as Awakening, it does initiate an automatic process which eventually leads to full Awakening. All saints have gone through this experience on the way to complete liberation. It marks the beginning of the end.

Q) What happens to identity as one grows?

A) As one continues the journey within, one's identity slips further into a vast ocean of light. Distinctions between objects blur. Gross sounds become less clear while subtle undercurrents of sound come to the fore. Breath ceases spontaneously, even with eyes open. Ones identity becomes immensely vast. All beings become like your own children. There is a growing sense of love and protection. Silence is now so profound that even in movement, nothing moves anymore. It is all so beautiful. I am now just a tingling ocean of consciousness. It is beyond human; more towards Divine.

Q) Would you discuss what happens when the Self is realized?

A) At some point, through the Divine Grace, one comes to the realization that one is the higher Self. The identification with the Higher Self becomes complete. A merging takes place and one then no longer feels driven by the small self. The merging is experienced as an extremely powerful surrender. Everything inside and outside becomes very silent. Within this silence is the very subtle movement of the Cosmic Plan. There are soft, rolling pulsations of bliss ebb and flow on their way across the Universe. These pulsations are the Self-interacting dynamics of Consciousness. But it is the Great Silence which animates these creative pulsations. It is a different kind of silence. It is so silent that the only way to notice it is through movement within itself. God lives here. God is in charge. Ego can't exist here. One just has to surrender to it. One becomes none. One comes out of the experience knowing that something fantastic just happened, but there are no words to describe it. The proof is in the support of nature in everyday life. Life becomes wonderful. Sharp edges get rounded. There is lots of joy. Life is lovely and compassionate; fun and interesting.

Q) What is right action in the state of Awakening?

A) In this state, there is an overall knowingness of how things work. There is a subtle knowledge here that does not occur in "normal" waking consciousness. One just knows without an intellectual process. I am here, floating in eternity. What needs to be known will become available to me without any effort. True knowing only occurs in perfect silence. The mind must be still, so still that everything else in ones awareness starts moving. One remained fixed. The rest moves. Movement and knowledge are one. When one sees the true nature of his/hers creation, the right action in each moment is assured. Right action does not always mean good, happy or constructive. Right action simply means correct action for the moment. Any action may be correct in the truest cosmic sense. In the end, it is easy to do good. It is far more difficult to do what is correct. Correct may not be popular. It may not be pleasant. It is just perfect for you and your world. Christ, Gandhi, and Martin Luther King were correct even though their right actions resulted in their deaths.

Q) Why is it so difficult for us to understand the experience of Awakening?

A) The interesting thing is that no one can understand this experience unless they are in it. That is Nature's trick and that's why it is so hard to get. The great texts of all religions allude to it. It can't be seen, heard, touched, etc, yet it is the only real experience a soul can achieve. You can't share it with anyone. They all think you're crazy. They think that you are suffering from some sort of delusion. They can't see a difference from how you were before. But the fact is that the experience is real and it is they who are not.

Q) How can we best use Shakti or spiritual energy?

A) Shakti must be pulled up and in. Normally, human energy goes down and out. It is a cognitive choice. The correct thought and attitude produces a change in the direction of the spiritual energy. It is automatic. We come hard-wired for this. So let go, disconnect, and go up spontaneously. Let it go! Let the world off the hook. Listen to the high truth. It's like a radio station in the sky. A chain reaction will then take place. The Self will begin to collapse upon itself. Your light will never again escape. You will implode. You will cease. You will cease, yet all will remain. Pray for Grace to help you do this.

Q) Can you tell us more about your book?

A) Some aspects of this book are deeply personal. Why? Awakened souls are also still in the body. Our bodies are filled with lifetimes of experiences. The Awakened actually feel a lot more than the "normal" person. The Awakened can have families. The Awakened sometimes get sick. The finances of the Awakened can go up and down just like everyone else. So why get Awakened? To feel at home, that's why. You will never ever feel lost again. You will always feel connected to the source. An intimate bond always connects you to the Creator. People will still love, hate, or be indifferent towards you. But now the whole drama of life takes place within your own consciousness. Nothing can occur that is not you.

Q) Tell us about the Crown Chakra. What is the value of opening it?

A) Big power starts with the opening of the Crown Chakra. Huge waves of universal energy pour through into the earth plane. One feels like a divine light plugged directly into God. The energy in the crown seems to be increasing logrythmically. The crown turns out to be a tube of light which extends out to a series of universes made out of fine light. All human archetypal knowledge trickles down to us from these high spiritual planes. The crown energy is very different. There is no earth energy at all. It is completely spiritual. It is filled with dieties, devas, and holy beings of all kinds. Above the crown is the light of God. It is egoless. It is an awesome power. From this level, life is just a dance. You have little to do with what you do. It just gets done. There are no distinctions.

Q) How do the stars and planets affect us?

A) Knowledge is "in the moment" and is directly related to the position and motion of the Celestial Bodies. So Knowledge is different in each moment. Knowledge is constantly in motion and it is constantly being pulled. Therefore, because Knowledge is so fluid and vulnerable, we can never really be certain of what we "know".

Q) What are Siddhi Powers? Are they a measure of Awakening?

A) Siddhi Powers have long been employed by Yogis to make the best use of their time and energy. Yogis were the first efficiency experts. Siddhi Powers are shortcuts. Think of them as pathways, back doors, connecting a particular cause with a particular effect. All Siddhi Powers originate in the Chakras. Siddhi Powers are expressed in the sound "Ah" and are related to light. They represent enhanced mind/body coordination. However, Siddhi Powers are not Awakening. They can actually impede an Awakening.

Q) Who am I? What is my relationship to the world?

A) The truth is that Creation simply interacts with itself. "US" is a notion. There is really no "us". We are really just one witness with multiple points of view. We are Consciousness only. I can feel the Universal Soul animating my body. It swims. The Soul enters the world through my senses and my experience. It is my mind which encourages my Soul to identify with the body. Enlightenment is just re-identification with the Soul. When I directly experience the Universal Soul animating my body, I wake up to the truth that I am not the body. I am that which animates it. I am the experiencer. I am here on earth to experience my Self; to glorify my Self. I will never die because I am not of this impermanent world. The world happens to itself. It is an archetypal misconception to believe in any part of this world as my own. After all, How can I own what can never be mine? Because my thoughts are not mine and I use thoughts to evaluate my world, I am a victim of misinformation. My thoughts, my actions, my interactions, my perceptions are separate from my Soul; from the real me. They are unreal. They are, at best, constructs, notions, interpretations of a "reality" which is apart from me. Life interacts with itself, only. I am just the Witness.

Q) How is the mind related to the moment?

A) The mind creates discontent. The mind convinces us that something is missing. The mind convinces us that we are essential to the moment; that is, the mind convinces us that the moment is incorrect without our intervention. This is a false notion. Next time you feel that you must intervene in a drama, DON'T DO IT. Walk away. Just for once, walk away and see what happens. What will happen? The moment will happen. The moment does not need your assistance to take place. Nature is sufficient, on its own, to solve any problem. We are unnecessary to life expressing itself. Yogis experience this directly. They live a life of incredible freedom. They see that life happens to itself by itself. So Yogis don't get involved in the drama. Become a Yogi. Become a Witness to your life.

Q) How can I learn to see God?

A) Our mind has to stop moving. Then we will start to see God. We will see God as pervading everything. We will begin to experience the authentic Self in everyone and we begin to see that there is only one authentic Self in a myriad of different forms. For lack of a better name, we call it God. We will start to desire to know the Creator because we will be so in love with his/her creation. Soon, this desire becomes so strong that we must seek her out. Finally, we meet and our admiration for the Creator will be so strong that we will wish to become just like him/her. There will be a merging which takes place and we will become one with the Creator. This is the process of Unity. Then we come to realize that this is all nothing but ourselves. The more we receive the Oneness Blessing, the more this experience develops.

Q) Can you discuss action in the moment? Isn't good action better than bad action?

A) The effect of action is inaction. We act to rest. We give the mind a rest when we complete an act. But most of our acts are incomplete because we are not fully awake to the act. We should be completely open to the experience of every moment. Even while we sleep, we should be awake to the nature of sleep. Right or wrong, good or bad, have nothing to do with the true nature of an action. Being fully open to action is a value unto itself. Be aware. Look at yourself. Your body language says a lot that your mind won't allow you to express. A glance or a touch can say volumes about the moment. You have no control over how you behave. You can control it for a while, but, after a while, the truth leaks out. Your true experience cannot be suppressed. Gurus don't listen to a word of their disciples, rather they observe the disciples actions in the moment. Action alone circumvents the mind. If you forget to do something; if you are early or late, where you sit; how you sleep, a touch, a look, a smile, these are the only truth. They are direct channels of truth which link you to the Divine.

Q) What is the experience of God like?

A) There is only one truth. It is the truth that we are all

God. All actions eventually lead to this realization. But it is a very subtle truth and it is not available to the conscious mind. It is a truth that exists between thought and non-thought. It is neither, yet it is both. It is the domain of the paradox. It is an area of dynamic tension and non-directional flow.

Only Grace can create this experience. This experience, none of it, is describable through language. It is beyond space and time. It can't exist, yet it does. Our present reality is the child of this dimensionless dimension. Because of this, the potential to manifest any desire is inherent in the ability to operate from this space. Why is this? It is because everything in our universe is already there in virtual form. The experience is just incredible. It is as though you were sitting in a sort of "Cosmic Walmart", waiting to give birth to virtually any possibility.

What actually happens? I'm not certain. It appears that a kind of vacuum is created when one desires at this level. This vacuum-like non-space appears to disturb and restructure the matter composition of objects on the earth plane in such a way as to create the potential for the desired object to manifest.

It is a most unusual experience. I can't emphasize this enough. Sounds, sensations, thoughts, and feelings still exist, but there is no cognition, no connection, and no identification with them. There is only a sense of great joy and excitement, of enormous potentiality and deafening silence.

In Vedic philosophy, this area of experience is referred to as "Ritam Bara Pragya" or the source of thought. In Christian mythology, it might be referred to as the "Gates of Heaven". One literally stands with one foot on earth and the other in heaven. It is this point, where heaven and earth collide, that is the most fascinating. All of the Earth Plane qualities become infinite, limitless at Heaven's Gate. This is because the experiencer and that which is experienced seem to merge. The distinction between the "I" and the "Not-I" becomes unclear and oneness and unity dominate.

Objectively, certain changes, certain physiologic changes, occur during this experience. Breathing, that is, movement of breath stops. It is replaced by a fine coolness and "prana" surging throughout the body. The body tingles. Every inch is alive with a fine electric current. The body becomes rigid. The stomach muscles tighten. The spinal vertebrae pop. It feels as though you are dying. You are definitely not alive in the normal sense. One must be very brave to have this experience.

The true beauty of it is that one experiences eternity. It is no longer a metaphor. One ceases to be a victim of space/time and "forever" becomes a living reality.

Q) Describe Awakening?

A) There is a secret, inexpressible knowledge. In this state of Awakening, you are the answer. No speech is necessary-no action. Just be. There is nothing to do but make small talk. Just let them chase their dreams until they get tired and want to wake up. Then with a soft intention, you ask Divine Grace to unfold them. The God within them awakens. But you remain only as a product of their dreams. Your dream is over. You are their Self—their higher Self. They put you in their dream to remind them of the truth. They created you out of their own consciousness. You are their solution. Your identity only exists through them. You reflect them perfectly like a mirror.

Q) What is Karma?

A) Karma is action. Karma is a wave on pure consciousness. Good karma is that which tends to nullify the wave. Bad karma is that which tends to amplify the wave. The good or bad karmic waves expand out and influence everything in creation. Therefore, every action is felt by everyone and everything in creation. Karmic waves continue through life-times. They must eventually be neutralized. This is because all that can be known in the end is pure consciousness. Karma is the original sin. Karma is movement, motion, vibration. Karma is un-centering. One cannot exist on the earth plane without karma. Awakened ones have a karma. But their karma is a momentum from previous births. That momentum is kept alive through Grace. Grace is the magical action of God. God nullifies Karma through Grace. Dharma is directed karma. Action in one's dharma tends to nullify karma. Action in one's dharma creates coherent light. Light is both wave and particle in nature. It is only the wave nature that can become coherent. A wave is a virtual line in space/time. When a wave collapses into a loop, the result is a particle. Biological cells are round waves made of light. They are simultaneously between wave and particle. The double helix of DNA is male-female event. The essential constituents of the double helix, namely carbon, oxygen, nitrogen and hydrogen are qualities of expressed pure consciousness. They are directly related to creation, maintenance, destruction and the absolute value. DNA sequencing is expressed karma. The double helix strands of the DNA are two waves linked by a particle nature. The waves are like male and female. The particles are like children of the waves. Being centered is a perfect balance between the two DNA strands. Balanced strands create coherence. Coherent strands nullify karma. DNA sequence can be translated into sounds, elements, atomic configuration and weight. The Awakened sequence is perfect. At the level of balanced DNA you can begin to work on transforming the body into light waves. This would entail nullifying the central links between the DNA strands.

Q) Talk to us about Awakening?

A) When you are Awake, it's all there and dying to get out. It is all mantra. All becomes rich in cosmic purpose. There is an intense urgency to express. It is as if you might disappear in the next moment. You feel euphoric, limitless. It is as though you were creativity incarnate. You live and breathe the answer. God is seeping through every pore. You become divinity in matter. It is an unstoppable force. Nothing can possibly stop this expression. It is inevitable. It is nature's truth. It's all being expressed through each divine being. We are all divine channels. We are streams of consciousness, here to reconstruct the earth plane. We need Divine Grace. It is the only solution.

Q) Did the body create the mind? Did the mind create the Soul? Does the Soul have a biological basis?

A) These are the most fundamental questions. Most of our religious, philosophical, and societal structures are built on the notion that we are individual expressions of an infinite Soul. The Soul was the originator. The Soul is our true nature. We have all been taught from childhood that the Soul is boundless, beyond space and time, and lasting forever.

If the Soul is a function of the body and if Self-Realization, Awakening, is a realization of the Soul, it would follow that Awakening is purely biological. Awakening could then be reduced to a biochemical event at the level of the central nervous system and various structures of the brain such as the Pituitary Gland and Limbic System. Then the experience of Awakening, of infinite expansion, and ultimate knowledge, would appear to be a delusion. If the Soul has its origin as a byproduct of the brain or as a coping mechanism of the mind, then Awakening, Liberation, Self-Realization, Nirvana, Samadhi, Satori or sainthood would appear to be a self-induced, but very productive delusion. Then spiritual practices just modify biology and, in the end, we are all still victims of matter and eternity does not really exist.

My scientific, pragmatic predisposition was putting me in a precarious position. It all started to look to me like biochemistry. God, faith, devotion, and Awakening all began to look matter-based, biologically generated. Then something happened. For lack of a better word I call it Grace. Grace happened. My experience of the relationship of subject and object, of duality, just disappeared. In a flash, my conscious experience and the world that was constructed around it vanished. I vanished. And so did the dilemma. Here's how. I had suddenly fallen into a timeless, wordless awareness. My experience had become intensely immediate. Time outside the present moment had become irrelevant. Also, all points of view seemed to hold a common theme. Concepts like mind creating spirit or spirit creating mind now seemed at home with each other. I felt as though I could float in between opposites. Either option was now fine. It didn't matter anymore. Only the moment mattered.

Q) What is the value of silence? Are silence and mind related? Are silence and knowledge related?

A) The major point that people have trouble with is understanding that the complete knowledge of everything is available only when the mind stops, when thinking stops. At that moment, the perfect solution to every problem is available to us. All of the computers on earth running together could not form a more perfect solution than you can get from a silent mind. That is why we have to know nothing to know everything. We won't have all of the answers from all of the books yet we will be able to express perfection in every breath. And that perfection creates no waves. No karma is produced because it was not created by thought. When nature speaks to itself, there is no karma. Unless we become perfectly still inside, we will never know what is going on around us. Unless we become like the silent ocean, we will never know the waves. The Vedas say, "Knowledge is structured in consciousness". The higher we vibrate, the less we shake. The more silent and pure our vibration becomes, the more authentic the vibration of people and things around us becomes. We can then experience the authentic self of others.

Q) How did you come up with the content for your book?

A) Well, I didn't think about it or plan any of it. Really! The truth is that the sentences just kept appearing in my head. The interesting thing is that I initially experienced the sentences as groups of words without meaning. So, when I finally got back to read what I'd written, the words were as new and fresh to me as they are to you, the reader. When a holy person in India recently read "American Buddha", his only comment was the following, "You did not write this book, God did."

Q) Who am I? Who are you?

A) There is really no distinction between you and I. I feel you. I feel the starving souls in Africa. It wears on all of us; unconsciously of course. This is the universal uneasiness that we all feel. Even when we feel good, it is still there.

Q) How does Awakening affect those nearest to you?

A) Once you are able to sit in the moment, magic starts to happen to those around us. The impurities cannot remain long on those closest to us. It can be scary for them at times. Our friends may experience all sorts of emotional upheavals. But understand that magic can only exist where there is purity. Impurity cannot remain for long.

Q) What do you need? How would you describe yourself?

A) It is unnecessary for me to be saved. It is unnecessary for me to be loved, fed, clothed, sheltered, etc. I am not the body/mind. The body/mind needs things. I am that which exists without the body/mind. I need nothing. I am that being. I am essential to everything yet cannot be located in anything. The word "I" is just a symbol for the indescribable.

I am indescribable; even to myself.

Q) How can I evolve?

A) Evolution is a function of biochemistry. Evolution is really the evolution of the signals across the synaptic cleft. Good chemistry takes clean living. It takes low stress. Evolution takes surrender, deep rest, and diet. Don't suffer, but don't be selfish either. Do the things that your mother told you to do. She knew what was best for you.

Q) Will you Awaken me?

A) No! You will Awaken yourself. I will watch. I will cheer you on.

Q) Why are we not born Awakened?

A) What's the point? Life is school for ignorant people. Awakened people are like the senior class. They are ready to go somewhere else for higher education.

Q) What is karma?

A) Karma is your past and your future. There is no karma in the present moment. Past and future happen to you when you are unconscious. Be awake. Be free.

Q) My life is filled with suffering and turmoil. What can I do about it?

A) First, know that you chose it. This life is your deal with the Divine. Most of us bite off more than we can chew in this life because we feel such remorse for our past mistakes. So we try to resolve it all in one life. You can change your suffering in a moment. Divine Grace can rewrite your life now. Find Grace through Oneness Blessing. It exists and will emancipate you. It takes consciousness, focus, alertness, unbending desire, and a belief in the possibility of change. My advice to you is to walk away. Walk away from dramas right now. Don't waste time on distractions. Downsize. Simple and uncomplicated is good. God has blessed you with a certain amount of energy. Use it wisely. Follow your feelings, but always, always, always ask yourself how your actions will affect those around you. You have two bodies; local and universal. Your actions must serve both bodies. Finally, know you as God. Suffering ceases when you truly live this.

Q) How do I know that you can help me? I feel I know more than you do.

A) You probably do. It is not about knowing, it is about being. I can help you with this. I can help you to forget what you know.

Q) What is the most important practice?

A) Awake! Be awake to what is going on around you. Awake is not just one level. Many, many levels become available to you when you are awake to your own consciousness. You must train your awareness not to be lazy. Even when you feel lazy or sleepy do it with attentiveness. Evolution is just another name for increasing degrees of being awake.

Q) Who is the Creator?

A) Creator is your friend. The creator is in love with you; hopelessly in love. Creator wishes you all good. Creation is just the creator's toy store. And all knowledge of any of the creator's toys is available to you.

Q) What is the value of a Guru?

A) Guru is awake.

Q) Is eternity really eternal?

A) I'll get back to you on that.

Q) What is the solution to world peace?

A) World Peace is already within each of us. World peace can never be outside. So achieve world peace inside. The problem is solved.

Q) What is your basic teaching philosophy?

A) You must first forget everything I teach you, and then practice it regularly.

Q) What time is it?

A) It isn't.

Q) Where am I?

A) You're not.

Q) What is matter?

A) The gaps between space.

Q) What is infinity?

A) It is all relative.

Q) Who is God?

A) God is who is asking the question.

Q) What is the best advice you can give me?

A) Don't listen to me.

Q) How do you wish to be remembered?

A) I don't.

Q) What's your philosophy?

A) Your guess is as good as mine.

Q) What is important to you in the future?

A) I am not interested in tomorrow. Why bother? It will never be what I thought. Even the best tomorrow is completely unfulfilling. Sorrow is tomorrow. I choose Now.

Q) How do we become powerful?

A) Power comes as soon as you let go of it. You must disconnect to use it. Power is potential action. Learn to act. Learn not to act. Now, learn to act without acting. That's power!

Q) Should I change my diet?

A) It is not so much what goes in as what comes out of what goes in. A yogi can ingest poison and transform it into a life giving elixir. (Now, day old pizza may be another story.)

Q) How do I make my mind stronger?

A) A holy man's mind is very strong. The whole world may say he is wrong, but he will not be swayed. He will be right. His mind will make it right.

Q) Is there a group mind?

A) Yes, there is a group mind. The group mind produced motion within itself. This motion produced an infinite number of points of view. And each of these points of view has its attending thoughts. Therefore, each of our thoughts is just an aspect of the motion of one primordial group mind.

Q) Who are you?

A) I am my own self-contained knowledge. There is nothing else. I bow down and curl upon myself to create phenomenal existence. I am nothing. I am everything. I spontaneously move within myself to create the dream. I am that which is. I am in between. I am not yet. I am forever.

Q) You often say, "What is is". What does it mean?

A) Our mind will never allow what is. Our mind will always try to make what is not out of what is. Is is without color. Is is beyond interpretation. Is already contains what is. Is is everything as it is in the moment. Is is the blessing of the Creator. Is is Heaven on Earth.

Q) Would you discuss relationships?

A) They are out of our control. Relationships are God's learning tool. They create experience.

Q) Would you bless me?

A) I bless everyone I meet. You feel it now, don't you?

Q) How do I manifest?

A) Keep asking for what you want. All ladies know this. Men haven't caught on to this yet.

Q) What is the secret to life?

A) The great secret is that there is no secret to life. The secret is that there is really nothing beyond our personal experience. The secret is that our entire life is really in our own terms. This is why it is said that the goal of life is Self-Realization. It is the realization that our personal self is actually the universal Self. The personal self is truly universal simply because our personal experience is all that there is for us. Even the "Gurus", from whom we seek guidance, are really just aspects of our own personal consciousness. In the end, it's just us. Unfortunately, we all assume that there is some personal transformation that must occur before we can feel fulfilled. But nothing ever changes; not even a little. No matter which spiritual discipline we follow or how hard we try, nothing ever changes. It's always been the same. From birth, it's always been the same. All of our seeking has just brought us....more seeking. The permanent transformation that we were hoping for has never, ever materialized. Perhaps there was never any transformation possible in the first place. Perhaps there was really nothing to know; nowhere to go; and nothing for us to do. And perhaps just accepting this truth is the real meaning of Self-Realization. Is it so hard to believe that we are already complete? We have difficulty with this concept because we have been programmed to seek. Seeking has become almost a human genetic predisposition. On a deep level, we must come to experience that all of this is our own body and that there are actually no differences, anywhere. This change can only occur at the level of the neurophysiology. Oneness is a biologically based experience and it can only manifest through Grace. We must come to experience this Grace. We must come to experience ourselves everywhere. We must come to sense ourselves always. We must come to know that whatever we do, we are doing it directly to ourselves. We must come to know that even if the tiny aspect of ourselves that we call our personal self fails, a billion other aspects of ourselves are succeeding simultaneously. So we are always succeeding and, at the same time, we are always failing. This is because we are always the Universe. We are always the One

Q) How do I gain Enlightenment?

A) Frist of all, don't try to reach Enlightenment. You can't, because you already are Enlightened. We all are. The question really is how we got to the point where we began to experience ourselves as localized in the space of a body. This happens to all of us at around age one and one half. Before then, we are one with everything, everywhere. Everything is our own Self. But a perceptual flaw developed in humans probably 10,000 years ago that caused us to see ourselves as separate from the other after about age 1 1/2. For example, you see yourself as separate from you friend. That is where suffering starts. You feel separate from him. You want to help him but he is not you and therefore you feel helpless. That is due to an organic flaw in your brain chemistry. Meditation and yogic practices seek to remedy this, but with little success. There has to be a Divine intervention of some sort. God has to come from her side a pull you out of your ignorance. That is what happened to me. God pulled me out.

Q) Who am I and why do I suffer?

A) Your body is actually the body of the whole universe and it answers to God only. Your physical body is like a cell of a giant body. If there is a disturbance going on somewhere in the universal body, it may well be expressed through your nervous system or my nervous system as illness or pain.

Also, It is hard for us to understand that all of our experience is just neutral. It has no intrinsic value of its own. It is just happening. There is not good or bad experience. Experience is. We, namely our "I" sense, mistakenly identifies with the experience as our own. It gives value to our experience but this value is made up. Who is sick? Who is suffering? There is no localized who. There is a long standing defect in the brain which makes us experience ourselves as encased in this body. Same goes for the mind. Mind is not your mind. There is a universal mind expressing itself through your nervous system. Thoughts are from a universal repository of thoughts. They originate from every possible source. Let's talk personality. The personality who asked me the question will not be the one that thinks about the answer tomorrow. Personalities change like the weather. There is no core you or me.

So who is suffering and who needs healing? You do! Only the you that I am healing is infinite, unbounded and eternal. I heal your Soul. Soul is real. The rest is an overlay. I will pray for your Soul. I will heal your Soul.

Q) How do I train my mind to Awaken?

A) Awakening is not an intellectual pursuit. Awakening is experience alone. Usually, we experience three things simultaneously. We experience the subject, the object, and the medium through which we experience. When you look at a tree, there is you, the tree, and the medium of sight or the seer the seen and the seeing. Because we are wired this way, we can't really experience the tree. Rather we experience an interpretation of the tree. Now the tree is just "treeing", but we automatically embellish the tree with a bunch of different qualities. It is green, deciduous, branchy, red oak, and smells like pancake syrup. The tree is just "treeing". The Awakened just 'experience' the tree without any subject or object. The "I" is gone. The tree is not "over there". The seeing is gone. Just the experience of "treeing" remains. Awakening is not mental. You cannot think or "mood-make" your way there. It has nothing to do with mind or mood or feeling. The Awakened are not people with happy-faces. They are God. They are one with God's Consciousness. They are everything. They are you. They know you better than you know yourself. They are awake in your dream.

Q) What is the most powerful technique for manifestation?

A) You can have anything you want in this world as long as you are not here for it. What do I mean by this? Things manifest in this world for a purpose and things definitively do not manifest for a selfish purpose. The more "you" that is involved in your manifestation, the less support the "you" will receive. When the local "you" sense disappears, then the Divine simply becomes you. There is no more separation. The Divine works its plan through you. Divine timing kicks in and your life takes off. Then your life becomes a wild, wonderful and miraculous adventure.

Q) Why does Awakening take so long for westerners?

A) Awakening is actually a much slower process for westerners because we have been reinforced to believe that our God is only a punishing God and that, at a deep level, we feel that we can never be worthy of Awakening. God is neutral. God doesn't judge. We judge. The truth is that God spontaneously awakens whomever she chooses and whenever she chooses to do it. God does not keep a scorecard. I recently met a young Indian saint who used an analogy to make this point. He said, "The sun rises over the castle and the gutter in the same way. It is just the sun. It doesn't shine any brighter over the castle. Awakening is like the sun. Awakening is not a function of this world and it shines without any discrimination." He told me that westerners should learn to see God as their best friend and that God loves them so much and has been silently by their side guiding them all along.

Q) Are you an Awakened One? Can you describe your present experience?

A) This morning, I am observing this body of mine. These fingers are tapping on the laptop keyboard. Oxygenated blood is feeding the cells of the fingers. Electrical signals signifying the sensation of touch are racing to my brain. But something has happened to my brain. A functional shift has taken place. My brain is interpreting data differently. Now the tapping is perceived in a dramatically unique fashion. For lack of a better word, I would describe the new style of brain interpretation as Divine. There is a sense that Divine fingers are doing the tapping and that Divine nerves are sending electrical signals to a Divine brain. There is the sense that these physical processes are no longer the sole property of my body/mind. This experience is not an intellectual interpretation. Rather, it is a direct experience that I am living continually. It is an all-encompassing experience. That is, all of the data from my mind, thoughts, senses, personality and from the entire external world is immersed in a sense of unified wholeness that, to me, could only have originated in the Divine. This experience that I am living in is so wonderful but I just cannot express it to you properly because it is really not within the realm of language. The best way that I can put it is that my consciousness is just brimming with joy and intelligence. It is as if God herself opened the cosmic floodgates and heaven is just pouring through my body/mind. The holy ones from ancient times used words for it like Samadhi, Satori, Nirvana or Rapture. All cultures speak of this state and I can see that the great religions of the world probably originated in it.

ONENESS

In this Oneness, there is nothing different than my own Self.

I don't see or hear or understand anything other than this Oneness.

I'm not touched by thirst or hunger or sadness or decay or even death.

I'm separate from birth or youth or adulthood or old age or disease.

I don't experience myself as a body or a mind or a personality.

I'm beyond my occupation or my family name.

I'm beyond ideas like "I" or "you" or "this" or "that"."

I'm beyond good and bad, space, time, and this universe.

I'm beyond language.

I'm beyond activity.

I'm beyond consciousness itself.

I'm not the doer.

I'm not the experiencer.

I simply exist as the Self.

There is only the eternal Subject.

The objects have simply disappeared.

Through God's Grace, I've become changeless, limitless.

I'm the singular essence.

I'm that Oneness which appears as infinite forms.

Like ice, water and steam, which are just water, I remain unchanged.

I'm only that Oneness.

MY FRIEND

I have a friend.

She worries that I change my mind a lot.

I tell her not to worry.

I am the worry

I am the change.

I am the mind.

They are all within Me,

Like droplets of rain on a great ocean.

The ocean hardly notices

A PRAYER

I am the Universe.

I am every action, past, present, and future.

I am both knower and known; thinker and thought.

I am the Essence of Existence.

I am All-Inclusive.

Beyond Me, there is nothing.

I am Completeness.

Nothing can be added or subtracted.

Creation eminates from Me.

I am the Primordial Source.

I am the Creator.

I am both Father and Mother.

I am the Sustainer.

In the End, I will bring All back to Myself.

There is nowhere to go,

Nothing to do,

Nothing to be.

You are It already.

Run after it, It runs away.

Run away from it, It runs after you.

Just Stop!
Just Be.
Just accept that it is All You.
Just Play
And keep Dreaming.
And when you are finished,
Come Home

Appendix1

Oneness Blessings: Questions and Answers

Q) What do you advise people do while waiting for Liberation? I believe you had mentioned Oneness Blessing as a good choice.

A) Why wait? I don't understand waiting? It is foreign to me. It is the idea that we have to wait that is the problem. The present is PRESENT! NOW! HERE! It is the need to DO something (while you are waiting for what already IS all of the time) that is the cause of the problem. We have created an artificial gap between ourselves and what we already have. Don't wait. We are Enlightened right now. All This (everything that we are experiencing in the moment) is That (the answer). There is nothing "to do" here. Humans invented "to do" recently in our evolution. It didn't used to be this way. We used to not be so fixated on analyzing our experience. We just experienced. Why do we fool around? Awakening is only were there is no "to do". We need to drop the "to do". It's so simple. I believe in Oneness Blessing. It is a Gift. If you need "to do" something; I strongly suggest doing this.

Q) Does Oneness Blessing make it unnecessary to wait any longer?

A) Oneness Blessing will make you forget about waiting.

Q) How about Oneness Blessing, followed by techniques for specific aims such for health or for finances?

A) Intention Oneness Blessing would be the best approach. Aim the Grace, right from the source.

Q) What to do after Oneness Blessing?

A) Same as you did before. What is the difference? It is the same always. The moment is the same always. You must come to accept that there is NOTHING you can do from your side to make it better. Even your next thought is programmed. IT CAN'T BE CHANGED BY YOUR OWN EFFORTS. It is kind of like a drowning man trying to pull himself out of the water by tugging on his shirt.

Q) People want skillful ways and means to live a better life. If your "100 esoteric meditation techniques" will help them do that, then how would you feel about teaching them?

A) "Oneness Blessing" is the only consideration. "Oneness Blessing" contains the better life. It is the only skillful way. All of the rest of the mental techniques are temporary because they are "in mind".

For more information on the Oneness Blessing, please go to **Onenessmovement.org**

Appendix 2
SPIRITUAL TECHNOLOGY

Light Technique Introduction

I want to talk about Awakening. I want to discuss a technique specifically for Awakening. It is so simple. It is the nature of life itself. Anyone can practice it. The technique benefits the two worlds, namely, matter and spirit, because it links the two worlds together.

It is called the Light Technique. The Light Technique originated in South India. It is claimed to be one of the oldest and most powerful of the Siddha techniques. The Light Technique can be performed with eyes closed either sitting or lying down. It is a great bedtime practice. The Light Technique is also sometimes referred to in Ancient Texts as Yogic Sleep.

Here is the logic behind the practice. Physists tell us that we are all really made of light. Only the light has slowed down enough to create matter. Matter is just slow moving light particles. This slow light, in the form of our bodies, is the source of our personal Karma. This slow light is the source of our egos. So, it would be good for us to transcend this world of slow light. It would be good to get to a lighter world. The lighter the world, the less karma we carry. God, literally, is the brightest light. If we could become the most brilliant light we could imagine, like the Sun's light, we could become God. Simple! The ancient cultures of the East looked at the Sun and Moon and the stars and marveled at their brilliant power and purity. The Ancients also had a tremendous respect for their physical bodies as well and they concluded that the physical was one of many bodies that we inhabited. They believed that there were subtle light bodies were outside the restrictions of the physical body. The "Light Technique" utilizes this understanding of the subtle mechanics of creation.

Technique: Light Technique

Close the eyes. Imagine your physical body made up of just light particles. Now, imagine this "light body", which has no mass, and therefore weightless, rising up into the sky and then off into space. Imagine your light body going to the Sun. Now, you are at the Sun. Enter the Sun with your light body. The Sun's light is burning hot and of blinding brightness. Now, imagine the impurities in your body, mind, and ego being burnt up in the tremendous light and heat of the Sun. Continue to be there inside the Sun for some time. Allow the Sun to consume all of your impurities until all that is left is pure sunlight. Now you cannot be located anymore. You have merged with the Sun. This is the most powerful technique. Your life will change. Nature will come to support you more and more. A new and better lifepath will appear for you. The experience will be all-encompassing.

We are the children of the Sun. The Sun, Surya, is our link to the other world. The more we can see light, the higher our spiritual development will be. Awakening is just light in the Nervous System. Light in the Nervous System is just neuro-chemistry. When we imagine light, we pour neuro-chemicals associated with light into the synaptic cleft and any chemical "impurities", ie.,chemicals which resist light, are "burnt up". That is the scientific theory behind the "Light Technique". Let's face it. Light is Knowledge. That is why, when we shed light on something, it becomes clear. I recommend filling your Nervous System with light. Sit in the light often.

Technique: Present Moment

Have you ever just stopped? Just stop for a moment. Just be. Thoughts will come and go. Let them. Become aware of the ever-present Now. It flows. You may notice a flowing pleasant sensation. You could be here at least 5 minutes a day. Bring yourself, easily, into the moment. Miracles happen here. Miracles are just the children of the present moment.

Technique: Original Face

Here's a technique. Look at your face in a mirror. Make sure there are no distractions. Now look directly at the pupil of the left eye of your reflection. Relax, but maintain a passive awareness. Let thoughts come and go. Over time the face will naturally begin to change and become unclear. Allow this change to occur. It will come and go in waves. You are peeling away layers of your mask, deeper and deeper until your original face is revealed. You can perform this for 5 minutes a day.

Technique: Ah Healing Meditation

The "Ah" sound is the health sound. It is pure life giving energy. Use it to heal. Here's how. Put attention at the base of the spine. Imagine a bright light there. Think "Ah" as the faintest sound within this light. You could do this for 5 minutes. Now imagine "Ah" and the bright light gradually filling your entire body. You are filled with healing "Ah" light now. Using your right palm, lay your hand on the affected area. Ask the "ah" sound to provide you with the Grace to heal. Now close your eyes and allow the "Ah" light to pass through you. This technique is very powerful. The effect is an automatic reflex. You are not involved in the process. Dis-ease is just the lack of "Ah" light.

Technique: The AH Sutras

The following Sutras are designed to shift you into a Divine Consciousness. They can be either repeated slowly out loud (japa) or they can also repeated mentally (without moving tongue or lips).

Ah is the sound of light.

Ah is the hymn of the Kundalini.

Ah is the mother of all mantras.

Ah is the Creator God.

Ah, as a soundless sound, bestows the power to do anything.

Ah has no location and no limits.

Manifest creation is all a form of Ah.

This is an expression of Ah.

That is an expression of Ah.

Ah is revealing Itself to Itself through Itself.

Love Ah.

If you touch someone with Ah, their cells will transform.

Ah produces Soma.

Ah re-sequences DNA.

Ah is Om for the earth-plane

Ah is active Om.

Ah is male and female Shiva.

Ah is Shiva Androgyne: the Undifferentiated Source.

Ah lives at the Mooladhara.

Ah is the sound of Waking State.

Ah is the sound of the Now. Ah is neither subject nor object.

Ah has no qualities at all, yet it is all-inclusive.

Ah contains everything.

Ah and life are one.

Ah is the sound of intelligence.

Ah is Awake.

Ah is the source of sound and matter.

Ah mediates the gap between wave and particle.

Ah is the sound of the Divine plan.

Ah is the sound of Sri Chakra.

Ah is the seed of a billion mantras.

Ah is the great healer.

Ah is Guru in sound form.

Ah is the highest first.

Ah is Iccha Sakti.

Ah creates heat, light, and electricity at the nerves.

Ah burns past karma.

Ah gave birth to Gayatri.

Ah plus desire at the Third Eye equals manifestation.

Ah is the sound of the Now.

Ah has neither subject nor object.

Ah has no qualities at all. yet,

Ah is all-inclusive.

Ah contains everything.

Ah and Life are one. When Ah ceases, so do we.

Ah is located at the Mooladhara.

Ah is Shiva/Shakti.

Ah is the sound of intelligence.

Ah is the source of the Siddhi Powers.

Ah is Awake.

Ah is the source of sound and matter.

Ah mediates the gap between wave and particle.

Ah is the light of God.

Ah is the Divine Plan.

Ah is Sri Chakra.

Ah is all you will ever need.

Ah is non-local. It exists everywhere, simultaneously.

Ah is the seed of a billion mantras.

Ah is the Great Healer.

Ah, at the Mooladhara, bestows enormous power.

Ah should be entertained constantly.

Ah is Guru in sound form.

Ah creates heat, light, and electricity at the nerves. Therefore,

Ah burns up our past karmas.

All actions in this Universe have their source in the sound Ah.

The power behind power lies, coiled, asleep within the sound Ah.

Gurus spend lifetimes entertaining "Ah".

All Siddhi Powers emanate from Ah.

Waking State is a by-product of Ah.

All new life is an expression of Ah.

Ah is the primordial seat of the "Big Bang".

Ah knowledge pre-dates time.

American Buddha Chakra Technique

I want to teach you a technique that you can perform, quickly and easily, anywhere. It is based on a very powerful spiritual technology that originated thousand of years ago in South India. It involves enlivening the Chakras systematically and sequentially.

1) We will begin with the First Chakra, the Mooladhara Chakra, which is located at a point between the genitals and anus. This point is related to the physical body or Annamaya kosha. The mantra or sound for this particular area is the sound Lang, pronounced (Laaaaaaaaaannnnnnnnnnnng). Say it out loud for 10 seconds with your attention at this spot. Follow the same procedure for the other Chakras..

2) The second Chakra, the Swadishtana, is located at the genitals. It is another point related to the physical body. The mantra to enliven this area is the sound Vang (pronounced Vaaaannnnnnnnnnnnnnnnng) (10 seconds)

3) The third Chakra, the Manipura, is located at the Navel. It is related to the Pranamaya Kosha or Energy Body. The mantra to enliven this area is the sound Rang, pronounced (Ruuuuuuunnnnnnnnnnnnnnnnng). (10 seconds)

4) The fourth Chakra, the Anahata, is located at the Heart in the center of the Chest. It is related to the Karmamaya

Body or Karmic Body. The mantra to enliven this area is the sound Yang, pronounced (Yaaaaannnnnnnnnnnng). (10 seconds)

5) The fifth Chakra, Vishuddha Chakra, is located at the throat. It is related to Manomaya Body or Mind Body. The mantra to enliven this area is the sound Hang, pronounced (Haaaaaannnnnnnnnnnnng). (10 seconds)

6) The sixth Chakra, the Agneya Chakra, is located at the Third Eye (between the eyebrows). It is related to the Viganamaya Body or the Wisdom Body. The mantra used to enliven this area is the sound Om, pronounced (Aaaaaaaaaaoooooooooooooommmm). (30 seconds)

7) The seventh Chakra, the Sahasrara Chakra, is located at the crown (center of the top of the head and is in the form of a thousand peteled lotus). It is related to the Anandamaya Body or Bliss Body. The mantras used to enliven this area are the sounds Augum Satyam Om, pronounced (Ogum Sotyum Ooommmmm). (10 seconds)

8) Imagine a golden ball of light above the crown. (10 seconds)

The following constitutes one cycle of the above technique. About 2 minutes.

MANTRA	CHAKRA	LOCATION	TIME
Lang	Mooladhara	between genitals and anus	10 seconds
Vang	Swadishtana	genitals	10 seconds
Rang	Manipura	navel	10 seconds
Yang	Anahata	heart	10 seconds
Hang	Vishuhhda	throat	10 seconds
Om	Agneya	third eye	30 seconds
Augum Satyam Om	Sahasrara	crown	10 seconds
Imagine a golden ball of light just above the crown			10 seconds

(This cycle can be repeated up to 7 times)

After you have completed your cycles, close your eyes and put attention on the center of your spinal column from the based of the spine up to your crown.

Imagine a very fine tube in the center of the spine. Now, fill the tube with a golden light.

From the base of the spine to the golden ball of light located just above the crown, the fine tube, the Kundalini, is now filled with a golden light.

(Optional) If you wish, you can say a prayer, a mantra, to the Goddess of the Kundalini. It goes Kundalini arohanam, Kundalini arohanam, Kundalini arohanam.

Now, imagine the palms of my hands resting on the crown of your head. Imagine the light from the golden ball pouring through my palms and into your crown. It is filling your entire body with a golden Divine light. This is the light of Grace. This is the light of God. Sit quietly with eyes closed in this light of Divine Presence. You may lie down after a couple of minutes and just be with the body. This will allow the Divine Grace to integrate into the various subtle bodies. You can perform this technique every day.

NOTE: All of the above the techniques are most effective when used in conjunction with the Oneness Blessing.

Appendix 3
MANIFESTATION

There is a lot of talk these days about the groundbreaking book, The Secret, and about the process of the manifestation of our desires. It's a fascinating subject. But it is not new information. The Law of Attraction, namely, like attracts like, is a very old knowledge. The bible attests to this when it states, "As ye sow, so shall ye reap". What you do comes back to you. In India, there is the Law of Karma. It says that "Action comes back to you in equal measure. In Egypt, you have the Code of Hammarabi. It states the familiar, "An eye for an eye". If you do something, it comes back to you equally. Even in Newtonian Physics, action equals reaction. Basically, what we think is what we become. Another way of saying this is that we manifest what our attention is on. This has been the message of such great modern thinkers as Dr. Norman Vincent Peale, Dr. Deepak Chopra, Dr. Wayne Dyer, and motivational guru Tony Robbins.

Another point is that understanding the Law of Attraction is one thing, but being able to apply it in practical life is another. Here's what I mean. If my mind is cluttered with a bunch of thoughts, how can I maintain my attention on what I desire long enough to manifest it. Let me give you a specific example. Let's say that you and I and an Indian yogi, are hungry and we each put our attention manifesting a Kit Kat bar. What will happen? While you and I will remain struggling and hungry, the yogi will be enjoying his Kit Kat bar. For him, the bar manifested almost as soon as he thought the words Kit Kat. Why? The yogis' attention is powerful and unbroken. He has cultured his brain and nervous system to manifest his desires with great efficiency.

Finally, the manifestation of objects such as houses, wealth and relationships are fine in themselves, but they do not guarantee happiness. This is a point that the Buddha made thousands of years ago. He concludes that desire and manifestation were actually the source of unhappiness. The Buddha devoted the rest of his life to finding a way to get beyond the problem of craving and desire.

To me, manifestation is just the mechanism through which Grace enters our world. Manifestation is the relationship of the subject to the object over time. The reality, and I use the term loosely, is that all of the objects of our everyday experience, are thoughts that have turned into matter.

Today, I want share with you some of the secrets of yogic manifestation. To accomplish this, it is first necessary to acquaint you with the mechanics of the human mind. Let's begin with the term Samadhi. Yogis often use the term Samadhi. It is said to be the highest experience of yogic meditation. But Samadhi is not a useful state if we want to manifest our desires. Here's why. Samadhi is a state of perfect silence. In Samadhi, this world vanishes and only pure conscious (consciousness without an object) remains. Nothing is left. The state of pure consciousness is a state of no movement. There are no qualities; no subject; no object; no

STUART MOONEY

relationship. Unfortunately, no desire can be entertained in Samadhi and manifestation requires desire. MANIFESTA-TION REQUIRES A RELATIONSHIP OF SUBJECT TO OBJECT OVER TIME. Yogis manifest from within the sphere of matter and change. They manifest from a spot where pure consciousness turns into matter. I will teach you how to take your awareness to this point. I will teach you step by step how to manifest.

I am often asked the question, "Why can't I manifest"? The answer is that you are desiring your manifestation from a false sense of I. You see your personal "I" and the world that your "I" exists in as separate. So you believe that it takes a lot of effort to put your desires into this foreign land that you live in. In reality, there is no difference between you and what you experience. Both take place inside the real you. You could not exist without the not-you so the not you is you too. Feel it. Look closely. Be perfectly still. To do this, completely stop your eyes and tongue from moving. (Try this for one minute)You are the other as much as you are yourself. Neither can exist independently of the other. Desiring and manifesting are just two sides of the same coin. Become the coin. The object of your desire is just you in reverse. A yogi has no trouble manifesting because he sees that he is actually the object of his desire. If a yogi desires a Lexus, he becomes it. The yogi moves effortlessly between subject and object. The yogi is both because the yogi is One with all things. He is living reality. The yogi lives the truth.

A yogi's mind is very, very still. It operates in the gap between the mind and the non-mind. At this level, at the level of the gap, a yogi has no identity. A yogi has no sense of self. At the level of the gap, a yogi can imagine any object so intently that he actually becomes it. This is how a yogi can read your mind. He vanishes and only your mind remains. This way, the yogi can actually become you and know what you know.

There is a relationship between the mind/non-mind gap and the Quantum Mechanical Ground State: the purported source of the physical universe. Perhaps the behavior of the thoughts in our mind is related to the behavior of sub-atomic particles emerging from the Ground State. After all, thoughts occur in the physical universe and are associated with physiologic tags called neurotransmitters which course through our body each time we have a thought.

The common notion is that, if you are a yogi, you are one with all things. Therefore, the yogi would have power over everything in creation. Any desire they have would spontaneously manifest. This sounds logical but Natural Law is not based on logic. Natural Law is based on invisible principles not available to the mind. The yogis operate within these invisible principles. When a normal person entertains a desire, he/she experiences the desire in a personal way. It is "my" desire. There is a sense of ownership. I want this. I desire such and such.

The yogis operate from a different frame of reference. The nature of the desire has changed. This is because the sense of "I' or "mine" has become expanded. If one is a yogi, then life takes place INSIDE of you. Desire and the object of desire both happen inside of you. To the yogi, IT IS IMPOSSIBLE TO EXPERIENCE THE OBJECTS OF DESIRE AS PERSONAL DESIRES because there is an overriding ONENESS which pervades everything, everywhere. So the ability to put conscious attention on a "personal" desire is missing. The needs of the moment or the needs of nature become of overriding importance.

Manifestation implies action. Motion, mind, time, desire, and cause and effect are all required for manifestation. None of these qualities exist in Samadhi because Samadhi is outside of the mind. In the perfect stillness of Samadhi, something has to happen in order to manifest. Some disturbance has to take place and that is mind. Mind can only manifest. Mind has subject and object. Mind contains desire which connects the subject to the object. As Christ put it," Ask first, and then you shall receive. Asking requires a mind. Mind requires an ego and ego requires a subject desiring an object.

The interesting thing is that the manifestation is most where mind is least. The more subtle that the mind is, the more powerful is one's ability turn a thought into an object. The object could be a three dimensional object. The object could be as subtle as the thought of Love. There is a point where mind and non-mind interface. In the non-mind, there is only fullness. There is the potential for any possible manifestation in the non-mind. It is full of everything but it has not yet localized as any one thing. At the point where mind begins, non-mind condenses itself into a point of energy. We could call it a faint impulse without any qualities. Although it is localized, it contains all of the potential of the Universal non-mind still within it. The faint impulse is in the gap between the mind and the non-mind.

Now, I'd like to take a little time to discuss time. Specifically, why do our desires take so much time to manifest into a physical reality? I call this time lag the "waiting period" between a desire and its fulfillment. Mostly, life is about this "waiting period". We are always are waiting for something or someone. We are always wasting a lot of time. We are waiting for the rest of the universe to catch up with us to fulfill our desires. We wait all the time. We are waiting for our vacation, our retirement, for the meeting to end or for that slow stop light to change. We are waiting for that girlfriend or boyfriend. We are waiting for the rain, the sun, or the night. You name it. It is always something. Until, one day, we are waiting for death. And, there we are again taking our first breath. Once again we are waiting. We are waiting to be by our mother's side. We need to solve the problem of the waiting period. How do we do this?

First, wasting time is a mass hypnotic state. We have all unconsciously agreed that things take time. Second, a yogi doesn't have to wait. When a yogi wants something, it manifests. There is no time lag. There is no sequential thinking. For a yogi, the cause IS the effect. If a yogi wants a Lexus, it's there; period. There are no salesmen, no financing, no rebates, no break in period, no waiting and absolutely no effort. A faint impulse of a Lexus in the yogis' mind is all it takes.

It would follow, then, that we should learn to manifest the way a yogi does. To function like a yogi's mind does, we must learn to operate at the level of consciousness where a yogi operates. So, let's give this level a name. Let's call it the Causal Plane. The Causal Plane is heavenly. It looks like earth only bathed in a beautiful light. It is so beautiful. Everything there is so pure, so perfect. The mountains, the lakes, the trees, the ocean, the houses, and the people are so beautiful. There is no suffering because the bodies are made of a fine light. Thoughts, if any, are faint and pure. There is no ego there. When we desire on the Causal Plane, the Plane of finest light, the desire is both perfect and powerful. When we desire on the Causal Plane, we just have to let it go. The desire will then begin to fall through increasingly gross planes of existence. Each plane has its own world. The desire will finally manifest in three dimensions on our earth plane. When we have a desire on the Causal Plane, it will definitely manifest. Here are some ways to connect to the Causal Plane:

1) Receive regular Oneness Blessings. This will align you with the Causal Plane.

2) Desire and Desire and Desire! Think about your desire all of the time. Feel it passionately. Picture it. Picture it in your mind. See it. Taste it. Smell it. Touch it. Manifestation is an emotional process. Write it down. To write it is to manifest it. It is has started to become physical. Picture it after you meditate. Picture your desire upon awakening and before you go to

bed. Think it every time your phone rings. The desire will manifest. That is certain. But let's get it to manifest sooner rather than later.

3) Be totally awake to the present moment, with your attention at the Third Eye (between the eyebrows), as you picture your desire.

4) Speak to your mind. Tell your mind not to live in the slow time. You want your manifestation now! Your manifestation is going to happen for sure sooner or later. All of your desires have to manifest. That is Natural Law. It is best to manifest right now because right now is the opportune moment. Next lifetime, that Lexus may not be as useful to you. That is the problem. This life, we are manifesting our past life desires. Unfortunately, they are no longer what we want. No more waiting is allowed. Do this practice often.

5) Don't doubt. Doubt is the mind trying to slow your manifestation. The mind lives for unending drama.

6) We are manifesting our desires all day long. We desire to get up. We get up. We desire a shower. We take a shower. We desire a coffee. We make some coffee. The list goes on and on. These are "little manifestations". "Big manifestations" seem harder. Why is it harder to manifest a house than a cup of coffee? It should be the identical process. I believe that the mind is on its own. And I believe that the relationship of thought and matter does not directly exist. Rather, I have concluded that the matter world is on automatic pilot and that our control of it is really an illusion. This is why manifesting "big" things is so hit or miss. Manifesting your desires is wholistic in nature and I believe that prayer (connecting with your higher power) is a good adjunct to manifestation. This is because prayer transcends the independent nature of mind, thought, and matter. Prayer is just the Oneness speaking to Herself. Know that this is all Oneness. Oneness is both the desire and its manifestation. Oneness is the mediator between

the two also. Ask the Oneness, your personal version of it, for help with your manifestation.

7) Push your manifestation. If it is not there, just know that it soon will be there. Act as though your manifestation has already happened. Act as though it is a foregone conclusion. Tell everyone that it will happen. Picture your manifestation in your Third Eye. That is a blueprint thought. Now, fill the thought with light. Light is manifestation energy. Thought is fine matter. Light manifests thought into matter.

8) The first thought impulse is the most powerful. It is pure condensed manifestation. Be innocent with it. It is the perfect architects drawing with the perfect energy to manifest.

9) Now ask yourself, "Why do you want the things you want"? The Goal of all manifestation is happiness. If your manifestations are good for not only you but for the goals of the universe, only then will you feel true happiness from the manifestation. Only then will it be fulfilling. Otherwise, it is just another thing.

Recognize that we are manifesting all the time. Acknowledge the small manifestations that are occurring in your life all the time. Manifestation is the product of attention and intention. Rather than coming at manifestation as a lone person in a hostile world, recognize that you are Oneness. Your manifestations are inseparable from that of the Creator. All of your manifestations are co-creations. So your manifestations will only take place if they are meant to take place. All you are seeing when you imagine your desires, is your future. You will then recognize your desire when it appears because you have already seen it in your mind and know what it looks like. Manifestation is just tapping into what nature is going to do anyway.

Now, you need to clarify what you want to manifest. Get in touch with one thing that is really important to you—your heart's desire. Visualize it. See it in your mind's eye. Entertain the image with intention. A will is an intention. Intend an outcome. Envision a reality. Dream it. Your dream is a blueprint. Keep dreaming the same dream. Over and over, see it with your inner vision. Your dream is unbroken. Your dream becomes your reality. No difference exists anymore. You are your dream. You are no longer dreaming. You are awake in your dream. You are awake and there is no longer a dreamer. And there is no longer a dream

Techniques for Manisfestation

1) You can intend what you want. It's easy. The trick is to understand the mechanism of manifestation. Manifestation is intent plus leverage. Desire it. Picture it in your mind. That is intent. Leverage makes energy come alive. The leverage is the sound "Ah". "Ah" is motion, magnetic motion between the pictured desire and the physical expression of the desire. "Ah" lights a fire under the picture. The picture shakes. It vibrates and becomes unstable. The picture seeks homeostasis by becoming physical. It slows down. It becomes heavy and falls. The picture falls into the physical. It finally lands near you but you must look to find it. To you, the manifestation of your desire is a coincidence. But it is just the technology of intent and leverage and it is absolutely perfect.

2) Here is another secret technique that the Siddha Masters used to manifest their desires:

Put your awareness in the Heart.

The spiritual Heart is located in the center of the chest.

Within the Heart, there is a light more brilliant than a million Suns.

Close your eyes and experience it now.

Within this brilliant light, there lives a beautiful Divine Being.

This Divine Being oversees all of Creation.

All of manifest Creation is an expression of the intent of this Divine Being.

Now, this Divine Being is awakened within you.

And because the Divine Being is awakened within you,

Your dreams will come true.

Imagine a dream.

Be very specific.

Visualize it within the brilliant light of the Heart.

Now picture the Divine Being blessing the image.

See it come to life.

Ask the Divine Being to manifest the image in your life RIGHT NOW!

It's done.

Be grateful

Now forget about it,

And go on with your life.

Appendix 4
THE STORY OF MEDITATION

There was a time when no meditation techniques yet existed. At that time, there were a group of yogis who sat quietly observing their own consciousness. They spent their time observing the three familiar states of waking, dreaming and sleeping. After some time, the yogis began to notice something. They observed that as one state of consciousness slipped seamlessly into another, there was a momentary gap.

The holy men investigated this gap and, over time, found ways of remaining in it for extended periods. They observed that the gap between waking, dreaming, and sleeping had a definite nature. They described it as being of infinite, unbounded, and wordless awareness. They described it as consciousness without an object. They described it as Pure Consciousness.

As they became more familiar with the gap, the yogis

found that it contained not emptiness, but rather a fullness which held everything in the universe within it. The structure of the mind revealed itself to these holy persons. They observed that each thought we have, had a source. They observed that thoughts emerge as an impulse out of Pure Consciousness. They observed that each thought expands like a bubble as it rises up through the mind. They saw that a thought, in its most condensed form, was the most powerful. They observed that the most powerful thought was right as it emerged from Pure Consciousness. It was the point where the universal Pure Consciousness became localized as a thought. They referred to this source of thought by the term, Ritam Bara Pragya.

As the yogis observed this source of thought more carefully, they saw 51 different sounds floating in virtual form in the Pure Consciousness. These were the 51 sounds that comprise the Sanskrit language. The yogis then observed that these sounds would combine in various combinations to form words. These Sanskrit words were observed to have a physical form within the mind. The name of the object created the physical form simultaneously. Another way of expressing this is that the sound value of a Sanskrit word at the source of thought would be transformed into a light value, the object value, at a less refined value of the mind. The yogis recognized a pivotal point where words turned from sound to light. They said that if they put their attention on the sound as it turned into a visual thought, the object would tend to quickly manifest into a three dimensional object.

Furthermore, the yogis then observed that there were Sanskrit sounds for each object in the universe. They referred to this as Nama and Rupa, name and form. The yogis concluded that everything in the universe existed as sound first, then as a three dimensional object. Their conclusion was that if they could manipulate the sound value of an object just as it became light, (light is the first matter) the object would manifest in the Physical world. All yogic manifestation techniques are based on this knowledge.

Now let's talk about mantras. Mantras are usually Sanskrit sounds although they exist in almost every language on earth. But they are not just sounds. Mantras are gateways through the fabric of nature. Mantras are deity sounds. Mantras enliven certain fundamental laws underlying creation. Each law is overseen by an intelligence that is often referred to as a deity. A female intelligence is used because the female is responsible for manifestation and creation. Female energy is active, moving and desire driven. Mantras tickle the deities. The deities love this. The deities in turn enliven the cosmic channels that connect the individual soul to the world.

Pure Consciousness has a tendency to remain outside of our three dimensional reality. Although it is the source and goal of existence, Pure Consciousness has to be harnessed or maybe a better word is stimulated. Yogis have long employed Mantras to tap into the tremendous creative potential of Nature. These mantras tend to localize Consciousness into very tight energy packets which can push our personal reality in various directions such as wealth, health, relationships or education. All of the mantras have a common source in the sound "Ah". Ah then divides into "Ah" and "Oo". The eternal subject "Ah" meets the eternal object "Oo". "Ah" and "On" the further divide into "Ah", "Oo", and "Ma". These three sounds combine to form the great mantra "Om". "Ah", "Oo", and "Ma" then divide into the sound of the five elements, namely, "Na (Earth) Ma (Water) Si (Fire) Va (Air) and Ya (Space). All of the other mantras grow from these five primordial sounds.

When we think the sound "Ah", we are actually thinking the sound of all mantras at once and we will receive the combined effects of these mantras. "Ah" is the archetypal sound. If we could come to experience "Ah" from its first intonation to its conclusion, we would have understood all that is understandable. All other sounds, and for that matter, all actions, would be completely comprehended. "Ah" is non-local, i.e., when "Ah" is intoned, it occurs everywhere, simultaneously. "Ah" is the creative mother. That is why we call mothers "Ma". "M" stands for matter. "A" stands for creation. "Ma" literally means Creative Mother. "Ah" and light are indistinguishable. As "Ah" manifests from the soul, it displays the most pure sound and most brilliant light. "Ah" can produce a tactile sensation, like a deep electric tingling as well. "Ah" can create a rich metallic taste, like gold metal, on the tip of the tongue. "Ah" can stimulate a cool minty breeze high up in the nostrils and, lastly,"Ah" is God in manifest form . "Ah" is the sound of the path that leads to the goal. It is safe to say that life is preprogrammed. Life's sequence of unfolding is flawlessly precise. Every little event fits perfectly into the innumerable events taking place everywhere in this moment. Again, the sequence is perfect. It was set into motion at the moment of the "Big Bang". The Big Bang created a sound, "Ah", and light. The sound, "Ah", created matter out of light by vibrating it and slowing it down. So the sound, "Ah" contains the exact sequence of unfolding of the Universe. Know "Ah" to know all. All relationships are "Ah" interacting with itself. All relationships are Shiva and his beloved Shakti. Both are the One. In the same way, "A" is Shiva and "H" is Shakti. Try to say "A" without "H". We can't. Being "Ah" is being the power to do anything, anywhere, any time. One becomes the building block of the Universe. Internal and external merge into a magical reality. Life is lived in a deeply symbolic manner. One becomes an archetypal embodiment. "Ah" is manifested Soul. "Ah" is the sound of light. "Ah" is the alpha and omega of existence. "Ah" is the dynamic tension which moves the beginning towards the end. "Ah" is the birth sound: the birth of the Universe, The birth of a baby, or the birth of an idea. As light moves into darkness; so does "A" move into "H". Ah is the sound of the soul. It is the source of tremendous power in this world. Heaven can only come to earth through Ah. Ah causes light to condense into matter. For instance, conception is Ah becoming localized in human form. So Ah can be thought of as the sound of life. Eventually, Ah will produce a stress free nervous system. Ah accomplishes this by its capacity to burn up impurities in the fine nerves that permeate the body. In India these channels are referred to as shrotas. Ah will continue to purify even after Awakening, eventually leading to a body made of fine light; a light body. It is a blessing to have the knowledge of Ah. Ah should be the faintest idea in your mind. Feeling Ah is far more powerful than thinking it. There is no limit to the intelligence contained in Ah. The great cultures of the world are but an expression of this sound. God and earth are linked to each other by the Ah sound. There is relationship between Ah and light. As white light contains all the spectral colors within it, so does Ah contain all of the primordial sounds of nature.

Oo is the sound of light-filled matter. Oo is the sound of heart-filled light. Oo is female Ah. Oo is Ah in two. Oo is the Unconscious. Oo is the Astral, Celestial, and Spiritual Planes. Oo is the end-product of Ah. Ah is the cause. Oo is the effect. Oo is the other great non-local sound. Oo bestows Enlightenment. It's true power can only be released when it is used in a non-verbal, non-thought form. Use it on the level of feeling, effortlessly beyond the mind. Oo is your heart. Oo is Parvati, Mother of Creation. Oo is the goal of Ah. Oo is the sound of the Dream State.

Oo is the heart sound. There is a lot of love and emotion in this sound. Oo is feminine and filled with desire. Oo creates attraction. Oo enhances intuition. Oo is the sound of the Feminine form of God. This Feminine form rules the world. The Masculine form of God is not active here. The Masculine form rules the Soul. The Masculine supports the

Feminine energy. The Feminine form is the cause of duality. The Masculine energy is subjective. The Feminine energy is objective. The Feminine form creates the dynamic tension between the subject and the object; between the cause and the effect. Love overcomes this primordial gap. Love is the Divine Union between the two.

Ma is localized Ah. Ma is Earthly desire. Ma is light stopped. Ma is dharma. Ma is the karmic wheel. Ma is Mind. Ma is located in the throat. Ma is your drama. Ma is the point value of Om. Ma is the sound of Deep Sleep State.

Ah, Oo, and Ma combine to create Om. Om is the sound of the Totality of Existence.

Om is the primordial source of the great Shiva Mantra, Na Ma Si Va Ya. Lets look more closely at these five syllables. The most important piece of information necessary to understand the Na ma si va ya Mantra is that each syllable refers to one of the five elements in Nature; namely, Earth, Water, Fire, Air, and Space (Akash).

Na is the Earth element. It is located at the Mooladhara Chakra. Na is the most solid, slow moving sound. Use the sound Na to make babies, manifest houses, buy land, do legal contracts, and to manifest jewelry, clothing and relationships. Na is the smell of the earth at harvest time.

Ma is the Water element. Ma is located at the Navel. Ma is Earth in motion. Ma is Na infused with air, fire, and space. Use the sound Ma at births, to manifest vacations at the beach and to manifest boats, jacuzzis, refrigerators, or a cool drink. Ma is the Moon. Ma is the Goddess. Ma always moves down.

Si is the Fire element. Si is located at the heart. Si is the Cause. Si is at the gap between matter and non-matter. Si is movement; restless movement. Si is always moving up. Si is Ma without Na. Use Si to manifest Cash, electronic devices, computers, a stove, a dryer, to manifest a new hair color or a name change. Hear the sound Si in beautiful flowers or a brilliant sunset.

Va is the Air element. Va is located at the throat. Va is the Space element infused with desire. Va is Sound. Va is the basis of Vayu, Voce, Vak, Voice, Volume, and Vastu. Va orients matter. Va is invisible yet felt. Va creates windy seas, flight, a soft kiss, the Springtime and the motion of the galaxies. Va creates intelligence. Va is the domain of the Goddess Saraswati. Use the sound Va to manifest a vacation in the mountains.

Ya is the Space element. Ya is located at the two eyes and the Third eye. Ya is not a localized sound. Ya exists everywhere, all the time. Ya is the God sound. It is the sound of the path. Ya is the last sound before Enlightenment. Ya is Sattwa. Ya is prayer. Your Guru is waiting for you in Ya.

GODDESS MANTRAS

The Goddess Mantras have long been utilized in India to stimulate various natural laws related to manifestation. They are a very powerful means to support desires in everyday life. Goddess sounds create a dynamic tension between subject and object. They create a magnetic attraction. These mantras or sounds are actually the most pleasing names of the Goddesses. Goddesses bless those who use their names.

Aim is the Saraswati Mantra. A= creation. I=intelligence M= matter/mother Literally, Aim is the sound of Creative Intelligence in matter. The Goddess Saraswati is the embodiment of intelligence. She oversees the natural Laws related to everything in the relative field of life. She rules over the arts, music, and all the creative domains. She can bestow Enlightenment so it is a good idea the gain her support. She mediates the relationship between a desire and its manifestation.

Hrim is the Parvati/Shakti Mantra. H=energy/power R=manifestation I=intelligence M=matter/mother The Goddess Parvati is the Primordial mother of the Universe. She is the power to move everything. She rules an unmanifest reality between Lord Shiva's perfect silence, deep and meditative, and Saraswati's knowledge of manifest existence. She, alone, bridges the gap. She is the lamp in the doorway. She eternally lights the inside and the outside. She is the link between God and man.

Shrim is the Lakshmi Mantra. S=ecstasy H=energy R=manifestation I=intelligence M=matter/mother The Goddess Lakshmi rules over the earthly joys including wealth and abundance. She makes matter pleasurable. She is the sensuous lover of the world. She attracts gold and jewelry, relationships, houses, friends, food and drink. She is the incarnation of the good life.

Klim is the Kali/Kama Mantra. K=desire L=emothin I=intelligence M=matter Klim is the sound of attraction. Klim is the sound of the Goddess of Desire.

Healing Grace Transmission photo taken in India, 2006

Look at my photo. Do this in a quiet atmosphere. Look into my eyes and relax. Let thoughts come and go as they wish. You are not your thoughts, anyway. You may experience many things as you continue to look at the Photo. There may be physical sensations. Perhaps there is some tingling up the spine or at the heart or even between the eyebrows. The Photo may change. Other images may appear. The Photo may even disappear into a white light. It doesn't matter. Just continue to look at the Photo, effortlessly. Do this for 10 minutes. What is happening? Grace is happening. Grace is restructuring your brain chemistry. Grace is restructuring your Destiny. Grace is structuring your Divinity.

Acknowledgment

American Buddha would not exist without the unwavering support of my best friend and spiritual partner, Irene Kokatay. Her insightful questions formed the basis for the book and I want to thank her personally. I want to express my appreciation to my parents for showing me what is truly of value in this world. I also want to thank my children, Josh, Luke, Chris, Eli, and Megan for their love for their dad. I also want to thank Irene's family and our joint grandchildren, Allison, Julian and Sophie. "Gwampa Stu" loves you. I have received support for this project from so many friends. Among them are Srinivas Ji, Krishnaraj Ji., Archarya Samadarshini, former DGP Sripall, S. Kumar, Betsy, Amber, Kimmie, JoJo, Russ and Avo and Arda Semerjian. Thank you. I want to thank all of my spiritual teachers including Mother Meera, Sri Amritanandamayi, Sri Karunamayi, Maharishi Mahesh Yogi, Helen and Charles F. Lutes and to my India teacher Sri Siva. And, most importantly, I wish to thank Sri Amma and Sri Bhagwan for the Grace which awakened me to Oneness.

About the Author

Stuart Mooney, MA has studied and lectured on the subject of the Awakened Consciousness worldwide for over 35 years. He continues to work tirelessly to spread the knowledge of Awakening through books, CDs, seminars and individual sessions. Stuart resides in Santa Barbara, California. Visit **www.americanbuddha.net** for more information on his work.